I0427246

OTUNBA JIDE OMIYALE
(MBA, FCIM)

PROFITABLE
SMALL BUSINESS IDEAS
FOR NIGERIA AND DEVELOPING
ECONOMIES.

'A Quick Start Business Guide To Fast Track You To Successful Entrepreneurship'

Dedication.

This book is dedicated to all persons striving to make the world a better place. Those who want to leave the word better than they met it.

Acknowledgement.

We acknowledge the assistance of https://www.freeimages.com/ for the images used in this work. And Google creatives.

Special Notice.

It's possible for readers to notice that this book has both British and American spellings.

Readers might, for instance, notice color in certain places and colour in others.

We humbly ask for your compassion in accepting both British and American spellings as being accurate.

Acceptance Of Responsibility.

We do not lay claim to any perfection, nobody is. Consequently, we accept full responsibility for any deficiency readers might find in this work.

We will cheerfully receive any suggestion to improve on this.

Legal Notice

While we have made all attempts to verify the information provided in this publication, neither the author nor the publisher assumes any responsibility for errors, omissions, or contrary interpretations of the materials here in this book.

The materials herein may be subject to varying state and/or local, and indeed, federal laws and regulations.

Before you commit resources to any project in this book, confirm the regulations guiding such investments from the local government level to the federal level.

Federal, state, and local government professional licensing, business practices, advertising, and all other aspects of doing business in the country are the sole responsibility of the purchaser or reader.

The author and publisher assume no responsibility or liability whatsoever on behalf of any purchaser or reader of this material.

This is material that any person can follow and be successful in business. Your success depends on your commitment.

Any perceived slights against specific individuals, professionals, races, or organizations are unintentional.

Contents

Introduction.

You are as good as what you have in your head.

A country does not become great because it is blessed with an abundance of mineral resources.

Were that to be so, Nigeria would be the greatest country on earth.

More often than not, the greatness of a country is a function of the optimization of its trained human resources.

That is why, when countries like Singapore, Israel, and Japan are mentioned, nobody remembers Nigeria.

Nigeria does not optimize her human capital; her youths are wasting away.

I know a couple of graduates who have been jobless for over five years; one of them holds a 2:1 in mechanical engineering.

This book is an attempt to assist people like these in starting up.

We all know the jobs are not there.

Are we now going to sit down and fold our arms, waiting for help we are sure will not come?

The answer is no, and therefore we should strive to help ourselves.

Self-employment is the solution, and this book gives you over a hundred possibilities.

Retirees and people in paid employment who want to start their own businesses can also use the ideas.

While on this journey, there are two problems you will face, and let me tell you from the beginning that the solution to both problems is YOU.

Capital sourcing, do you think?

No, I do not even consider that much of a problem because that will always be there.

There will never be enough of that, and if you are thinking of starting a business when you have enough capital, you will never start.

There are businesses you can start with zero capital.

Now for the two problems.

First, people around you will say it cannot be done.

They'll say it's impossible; no one has ever done it.

They will give you a thousand reasons why it will not work.

Remember, the cheapest commodity in this world is advice.

They come for free, and in most cases, they are worthless.

The answer to this problem is: do not discuss your idea with anybody unless you are sure the person will encourage you.

Edison said, "Tell the world what you want to do, but show them first."

The second problem is procrastination, the thief of time. Once again, YOU are the answer

Whatever you can do today, do not leave it till tomorrow.

Start where you are with what you have.

Do not bother your head about whether or not it conforms to people's expectations.

If you want to satisfy people, you will end up dissatisfying yourself and achieving nothing.

Most of the things we enjoy today were not available hitherto.

Some people dared to make them so.

They were discouraged and even persecuted, but they endured.

People like Euston, Newton, and Ford, the fathers of automobiles, and the Wright brothers, who first flew an airplane,

In this book, you will read about Nigerians who started with little or nothing and have grown octopus companies.

You will read of jobless graduates who took the world by the gullet and made a success of themselves.

All of them thought positively.

None of them took the negative advice, and all of them did things promptly.

You do likewise.

It is only you who can stop you.

I appreciate you purchasing this book, and I say cheers to your success.

Please send me a card when you arrive.

How To Use The Book

Your book, "Profitable Small Business Ideas for Nigeria and Developing Economies," is not an academic book.

It is written in such a way as to educate and entertain.

Therefore, my advice to you is to read from the beginning to the end in a relaxed mood, if you like.

There are reasons for this.

First, you get a general feel for the book.

Second, you may discover that some ideas are novel to you but may interest you.

Added to this are some inspiring stories embedded, which you may miss if you just follow the table of contents.

Having done that, you may now use the contents to reach the unique business ideas that interest you.

You may have hitches, and these are not unusual.

When this occurs, ask experienced people on the line questions.
Age has nothing to do with this; he may be a younger person who has been in business for a long time.

Last, I will always be there to assist.

Call me or send an email.

.

THE SME IDEAS

1.   Acting

The Nigeria film industry is just starting and for a country of 150million people, that should tell you there are opportunities in there.

Opportunities abound as actors, directors, producers, scriptwriters, costume and makeup artists and even singers.

Just last week Nigeria was rated the second largest video film producer in the world. This is contentious though, as some people feel that the rating did not take into cognizance the quality of the videos.

Notwithstanding, the money is there. If you have the talent, you can be an actor or actress. I must say that acting is more of talent than academic.

We must agree too that one will be a better actor if one marries his talent with education.

Many of the top earners in the industry today did not attend theatre schools.

Some of them attended their first audition by chance and they were picked and given roles ahead of theatre graduates.

If you have what it takes, just introduce yourself and interest to some of the practitioners and they will tell you what to do.

In Lagos, their rendezvous is the National Theatre and in Ibadan they have their office somewhere in Yemetu.

The interesting thing is that many film axes are springing up apart from Lagos and Ibadan axes.

Therefore, you do not have to come to Lagos to partake. We now have Kano axis, Jos axis, Abeokuta axis and others.

Like in all businesses, you need patience to get to the top. You cannot be Adebayo Salami (Oga Bello) Peter Edochie or Omotola aka Omo Sexy overnight.

You have to pay your dues or "carry forerunners bags" as I like to say.
If you are patient, and you put your all, the reward is worth it.
Entertainment pays and pays well.

2. Advertising.

I was going to title this advertising agency, but I thought I would rather not limit it to agency alone.
This is because; it has the inbuilt danger of limiting and narrowing the possibilities in the advertising business.

Know from the start that there are tons of money in advertising. I mean adverts on Radio and TV, on Cars and Lorries, on billboards, on house walls, on IBEDC polls and so on.

There is a new fad in town now to launch new products or to awaken awareness.

Boys and girls with branded shirts, dance on and around Lorries mounted with speakers blaring latest music in town.

Around and not far from the Lorries, others introduce or hawk the product.

Marketing professionals will call it sales promotion. Do not mind them that is for passing the examinations. To me it is all publicity and it is advertising.

Now, some people are organizing this and I have seen the big companies using them.

You can spice this up by adding acrobatic dancers.

The boys and girls are paid daily and you do not have to own the lorry and musical instruments, you hire them. In essence, your mobilization fee can take care of the expenses.

Another source of money in advertising is to register with media houses as an agent.

If you register with broadcasting stations as an agent, you will have some commissions given to you for adverts you bring to them.

 Now if you register with the government to consult on billboards or vehicles and overhead boards and banners you are on.

As I am writing, I am not sure billboards are thus controlled in Ekiti state. Surely, nobody is doing cabs ads in Ado Ekiti or even in Lagos

All those adverts on BRT buses can be replicated on the cabs. I am sure the situation is similar in other state capitals, so what are you waiting for? Explore the field of advertising and reap bountiful

3. Animal Feed Mill.

If some people are practising animal husbandry, some people must provide the feed. In addition, I tell you, many are making tons of money from this.

To have a slice you do not have to have millions.

Some hundreds of thousands of Naira will set you off.

The most important thing is to source properly and site your shop along a road accessible to vehicles.

The cost of the feed, freight, and other overheads will determine prices.

The big ones in the trade also influence prices to sell. Buy well to sell well.

You can even do this business without a truck as they bring some materials to you. Sometimes, you even pay after-sales.

Some of the materials you stock are Palm Kernel Cake (PKC), Groundnut Cake (GNC), Maize, Bone meal, Fishmeal, Brewery waste and Oyster shell.

You make distinct combinations to compound for Pigs, Fowls, Cattle, Goats, and Sheep and so on. Your area will determine what to stock.

Some things you may not survive without in this business are grinding and mixing machines.

The splendid news is that local fabricators make them and are not expensive. Prices are according to size.

You will also need strong young men to move and carry the bags if you are not strong yourself.

Even at that, you still need assistants. Scale, yes a scale is necessary but you can start with the cheap flat one.

One thing that will quickly grow the business is to give advice to farmers on their farms, especially feed substitutes and composition.

MARKETING: This is self-advertising. With your warehouse along the road, it cannot get lost and with wonderful service, farmers will advertise you.
Please do not use business names like Rise and Shine or Ogo Oluwa Feed mill. They sound very unprofessional. Instead, use catchy and refreshing business names.

Something like NOURISHING FEEDMILL, for instance. Instantly, the potential customer will be attracted because he wants his feed to be nourishing.

You can see, this name is relevant and easily remembered. Please read the section on naming businesses.

CAVEAT. Keep top quality feed. Assist the farmers; your success depends on their success.

Establish firm controls if you do not stay there all the time. People can be smart.

4. Bakery.

You do not have to be a millionaire to make bread.

Make special bread and people will beat a path to your place.

Bread sells. Not all those women along the road selling bread are there to enjoy the sun; they make money from bread and on bread.

You do not even need the local bakery to start. I mean, those bakeries made of mud.
There are people constructing bread ovens for as little as N30000. I know a woman here baking for soldiers at "Ojoo" area in Ibadan and she is doing well for herself.

The secret is a delicious recipe and good packaging. For packaging, copy the leaders like Leventis and UAC.

If you have a vehicle, it will expand your coverage but never mind, if you do not have, start and concentrate on an area.

For example, if you live at Jakande estate or Gowon Estate in Lagos, concentrate on your area.

To finish them, you can deliver them at their houses.

As long as it is ok and packaged well, they will buy.

Remember, when people buy bread, they buy the loaf and the wrapper.

 I must not deceive you and I will not.

You need to master your recipe properly before you hit the market. If you are not from a family of bakers, cut a cheque and learn.

There is no shortcut.

Do you know that there are many, making money from bread distribution?

Yes, there are. At Iloko, a town near Ilesha in Osun State, Oba Olashore bakes bread that sells as far as Ibadan and Ado Ekiti. Leventis and UAC bread are sold in Ibadan.

With time and better infrastructure, Lagos bread will be eaten in Maiduguri.

It is bread, my brother, everybody eats it.

MARKETING. Philip Kotler, the father of modern marketing, cannot sell an inferior product and bread cannot be different.

Make a good loaf, package it well within reasonable price range and that is it. Having done that, visit your locality with handbills, possibly with small samples.

You want a name, ok, JOY LOAF or BLESSED BREAD.

CAVEAT. This is food, please be neat.

To stand out, have a white overall with your brand name neatly inscribed at the back with red colour.

The overall is necessary for whoever is distributing. Minor things like this matter and make the difference.
If you have the misfortune to make poor bread, do not send it out. Destroy the lot.

5. Bank Accounts Reconciliation.

You cannot believe how banks are ripping off people, especially the rich illiterates.

They overcharge them on COT, OD, VAT, interests, and so on.

Do not believe that they spare the enormous companies. They also rip big organizations, even a behemoth like NNPC.

If your account is buoyant and you do not reconcile regularly, it will tempt them.

So Accounting graduates get your pencil and paper and reconcile accounts for rich market men, women, and organizations using bank facilities.

I must add that non-business related graduates can do this job if such persons are interested enough.

All it takes is a bit of tutelage or you collaborate with an experienced person and learn as you progress.

There are tons of money in this business, as you charge a commission on fund recovered, usually 10%.

If you recover Ten Million naira, your take will be One Million Naira, which is not small money.

The thing is that you can recover much more depending on the size of the account.

I know guys who have recovered over M50m on an account.

This is very easy because you will check the past ten years at least.

Now if the bank had been overcharging COT by N10, 000 naira every month for the past 10 years that is N1.2M.and some accounts are much bigger than that.

Besides, you have not seen the OD and the VAT.

There are many charges these days, which will be reversed if you protest. However, how many care to look at their accounts, let alone protest.

The banks wake up one day and just splash N100 debit on accounts and call it one banking jargon.

Imagine that in thousands of accounts, no wonder they grow fat necks.

Over 90% of Bank customers do not know how COT is calculated. If you doubt me, ask 10 people.

You will discover only one knows, if any of them knows.

If you do not know, as of today, it is N5 on every N1000 withdrawal while the VAT is 5% of COT. (Find out the current rate)

Overdraft and loan charges depend on agreement between the bank and your client.

We have put too much trust in the bankers. These days, their words are no more their bonds, so check their postings.

The joy in this business is that, for now, you do not need any licence or membership of any professional organization to practise.

Know the rules and make sure the banks follow the rules.

That is all. The rules are in the annual CBN regulations, which you can get free.

Get into this business quickly before the Accountants cartel it.

Now who are your potential customers?

I will say anybody just about anybody but I advise you go after high net individuals and organizations because the energy you will spend to recover N10,000 for an average man may be more than what you will use to recover one million Naira for a big account.

Having convinced your client, the first thing he does is to give you a letter of authority to look at his accounts.

He should send a copy of this letter to the bank.

 In fact, he should write a separate letter to the bank saying he has authorized you to look at his books.

You will now write officially to the bank saying you are representing so and so, attaching a copy of your client's letter.

The best is for you and your client or his recognized representative, usually the Accountant to visit the bank.

From that moment, the bank reveres you.

Now, do not ask me why the need for reconciliation when the organizations have accountants. Me I don't know, but money is there.

MARKETING; Your office and letterhead must be exquisite and you must dress well, probably better than the bank manager himself. You cannot afford to be Slovene.

Use your letterhead to introduce your outfit to prospects and follow up. One good account is all you need to be on the gravy road. You do not believe me.

Ok, talk to organizations, local governments, parastatals; you will be surprised at the amount of money to be made. Please, this is not a handbill business.

If you approach me with a handbill for a business of this importance, two things will come to my mind. The guy is either a nut or is doing a wrong job.

CAVEAT. Do not connive with the bank to rob your client because they will approach you to compromise. Do not do it, your loyalty is to your client. .

6. Beer Distribution.

Please see beer joints.

This business will serve the beer parlours and the public, especially when they are throwing parties.

It is equally lucrative but you will need a vehicle. You are a distributor while the beer joint man is a retailer.

Immediately, it should occur to you, you will need more money to do this one.

You will need a shop for a start and empty bottles, except you are a major distributor.

In that wise, you must have paid for the bottles as part of the distribution fee.

Attach yourself to a major distributor, buy from them and distribute.

You already have beer joint customers and as you ply their route, you honk to them and they buy, as they need.

Most times you come back to collect money when they have made sales. It is not that some will not be coming to your shops to buy.

Sometimes, your customer may book on the phone. In this business, there is not much margin, but you can make a decent living and it can even make you very rich.

Unlike the retailer, the cash you handle daily is larger and a small percentage of large is large. Currently, you make like N50 on a carton, If you sell 100 in a day and deduct the cost of fuel and servicing of the vehicle; it still leaves you with a tidy amount.

Do not be discouraged if you do not have a vehicle. Just position your shop in such a way that many beer joints, to surround where they will not need to board a vehicle to reach you, everybody is trying to cut cost you know.

An example of such a place is a motor park such as Ojota in Lagos or Iwo Road in Ibadan.

Apart from beer sellers, you may also supply those having parties. Since you have a vehicle, you just drop the stock. Do not forget to charge for transportation though.

MARKETING. In the beginning, move round to tell existing beer joints about your set up. As soon as a new one springs up in your territory, pay him a visit.

Your business depends on their success, so help them succeed.

I need not tell you that the shop must be where vehicles can easily load and offload.

CAVEAT. Watch the credit sales. If he does not pay for yesterday's purchase, no dice.
Be careful about how you handle money. Remember, people know you are handling a large amount and when.

7. Beer Joints

God forbid, if they are killing people at Yaba bus stop in Lagos, people will drink beer at Jibowu in the same Yaba.
There can never be enough beer parlours. More people are drinking and people are drinking more.

You do not believe me, have a look at the Profit and Loss Account and the Balance sheet of Nigerian Breweries and Guinness.

You cannot blame people for drinking, things are hard, and believe it or not, Nigerians are cheerful people.

We know how to make ourselves happy and that is why we are tolerating all these inept governments.

In this biz, the day you open, you make money. Get your shop, two sets of tables and chairs.

The joy is that you can take the drinks on credit and pay the following day. If you do not have a freezer, start with buying ice blocks.

You will end there anyway with the present power supply.

You need a piece of sublime music set to give you a wonderful start. TV reduces the sale of beer, music increases it.

That is the law, do not break it.

You may put on the TV during football matches to attract people, but those who watch TV drink less.

Because they have to use their eyes, TV takes their attention from the beer but pleasant music stimulates drinking.

A generator will improve sales and luckily, there are small ones going for about N10, 000.

The location must be accessible by car.

In addition, be nice to people. Nobody wants to spend his money under stress when he made the money under stress.

Support it with pepper soup to demand--Fish, Snail, Snake, yes Snake pepper soup. Study your customers, they may like Cowhide with pepper.

Before you introduce a product, ask your customers. Do not be a jack-of-all-trades.

If you want to pick fish, pick fish. Unless you are a limited liability company, you will need to join their association in your area, but then why not?

MARKETING. No fuss, the best advertisement is word of mouth. Tell friends to tell their friends.

As long as your service is good, they will come. If you do not see a regular customer for two days, phone him.

The profit on a bottle will take care of that and he will drink more than a bottle when he resurfaces. Such a customer will be glad you recognize him.

Everybody wants to be recognized, you know. During festivities, give presents to regulars.

CAVEAT. Never argue with a customer who has had one bottle too many.

Placate him. Never argue with any of them, drunk or not. In the beginning, if you drink beer, God saves you, because it is only God who can save you.

If you drink a bottle of Guilder, you have taken the profit on six bottles. Reserve your drinking until when your business can afford it.

Do not inflate your customer's bill. Be careful on cigarettes, it causes arguments.

When in doubt, resolve in favour of your customer. He will come back. A liquor licence is necessary

8. Bill Pasting And Distribution:

I once tried to paste some posters on my own, it did not take me 30 minutes to find out it was not a job for everybody.

I am therefore not surprised that the business is booming.

It has to, with politics and religious groups all over the place struggling for people's hearts.

This business does not need special skills or education, except that you have to be streetwise.

You must know the terrain, the culture, and the geography of the area to cover.

Your customers are legion.

The churches, the mosques, the filmmakers and their distributors, the musicians, the politicians, the government at all levels, schools, etc.

You must have a respectable office where they can call on you easily.

Normally, your charge will depend on the quantity, the area to cover, and where.

Price in Lagos per thousand will differ from that of Asaba for obvious reasons.

You will definitely need labor who will help to distribute and paste, whom you will pay per copy or per day.

In this business, you must set up a control system to stem the practice of dumping fliers without pasting.

Drive round to check or send ghost inspectors.

You must sensitize your workers to the effect that your success depends on the success of your clients and therefore they must do an honest job.

Confidence in a person does not prevent control, even with the talks, still, work your control.

MARKETING: Big road banners across busy roads and posters will do. Having secured a job, please do it well.

CAVEAT. If you have collected money from a man, do his job and do it well. Do not dump his materials.

9. Biography Writing.

I have deliberately taken this out of writing because of its specialty.

It brings money promptly, and in bags too. We are working on one factor.

Nigerians want to be celebrated even when they are just a little above mediocrity, not minding if they have contributed anything to society.

Not that there are not those who deserve to be celebrated. Jesus, there are many as you shall see.

The specialty of this form of writing is that you will not make your money from sales alone but also launching.

The first thing is to pick a principal, get his approval, and you are on.

You will need to get information from his associates and so the approval may be in writing.

The joy is that your principal may even fund the writing. If your principal is very marketable, publishers may sponsor the writing.

Who are the likely principals?

Your first choice is politicians.

They need such books to boost their political standing if they merit it.

The businesspersons are also suitable materials.

We are not talking about businesspersons without offices.

You would want to write on people with a network of wealthy people who are willing or can be easily intimidated to honor him.

The president, for instance, is a sure bet if you are close enough.

The VP, your governor, his deputy, your senator, the assembly member, the king of your town. Businessmen like Dangote, Femi Otedola, Jimoh Ibrahim, Osage. Oviah, the Zenith boss, Onosode, Christopher Kolade, etc.

Any book on any of these will make you an instant millionaire if marketed the right way.

For the latter group, such books will make money in launching and sales, but the politicians are not likely going to fetch much after they have left office.

Look, even if your English is not good enough, you can commission a talented writer to do it for you. It is a matter of cash.

As you will see elsewhere in this book, all you see in speech deliveries are not real.

MARKETING. The publishers are not new at marketing. Talk to the publishers and take advice from journalists.

Titling the book captivatingly may yet be the greatest task you face in the writing.

The title does matter a lot, not only here but also any book you may write. Sometimes sales increased by 1000% with just the title changed and the content intact.

Even if the book is not so good, it has to be titled captivatingly and marketed appropriately.

The launching has to be timed properly, and those invited must be given adequate notice and be reminded until the D-Date.

Please pick your principal with care, one mistake and you get a flop.

CAVEAT. Get your facts right so you do not transfer your profit to lawyers. Pick your principal timely.

I doubt if a book on Chief Obasanjo will attract much crowd today for obvious reasons.

Anyone on Buhari now will sell and may not fetch much when he leaves office. Books on Dangote or Otedola will be profitable because Nigerians love them.

If somebody writes a book sounding like "From N0.5M to N 400 Billion, the story of Dangote" I will buy the very day it is out.

10. Birthday And Wedding Cakes.

Daily, people both young and old celebrate birthdays and consummate marriages.

On both occasions, cakes are specially made, and it is increasingly being made in special ways.

In addition, corporate citizens have one thing or the other to do which involves the need for cake.

Ask Mojisola Egbeyemi who abandoned the wig to start a cake business, she will tell you how sweet the business is.

Anything you desire with passion will surely earn you money.

Cake business has become art not meant for everybody.

If you can gain the skill and make special cakes for these special occasions, you can make very well for yourself.

Happily enough, the materials are readily available. What will distinguish you is your creativity.

The other day, I attended a marriage ceremony, which had a special cake and the cake maker had to explain the significance of the cake.

According to her, the green color represented the profession of the husband which is agriculture.

She also had some other things for the wife and so on. I was impressed and wished the cake was not eaten.

The cake did not cost peanuts.

Because creativity is being paid for here, the price may not vary directly as the price of the materials used, however, you must price in a way to cover all your costs.

One enjoyable thing in this business is that they pay you in advance, but this should not encourage you to do a shoddy job.

If you get to make the cake for the birthday of an octogenarian with rich children and you are creative, you can be sure of smiling to the bank.

MARKETING. You will need a cute business card to hand out to people during parties.

Do not miss the opportunity of advertising yourself through the MC at any party you have made the cake.

Also, use church societies to propagate your business. I do not have to tell you to be friendly with unmarried people and those who may need cakes to be made.

For a start, you may work from home but ultimately you will need a befitting office.

CAVEAT. Agree on ideas before you make the cake and make sure you get the last nod of your principal before supply and please supply to time.

It is worthless bringing the cake when the marriage is half done. The cake should wait for the celebrant.

11. Block Making.

Let cement sell for N3000 a bag, people will still build houses, and the government will keep improving the present infrastructure.

For now, the cement block has not gotten a replacement. Block making is a lucrative business and the pieces of evidence are around you.

One advantage here is that labor is not permanent; you do not pay them when they are not working.

We pay them according to the number of bags of cement used.

Location is very important in this business. It must be on a major road that is easily accessible.

There are reasons for this. One is the ease of transportation of both raw materials and the finished products.

The second reason is that block business is self-advertising. It has to be in a place where potential buyers ply so they can see your setup as they pass by.

It is very usual to establish block making in a developing area for people constructing houses.

The economists call this nearness to market. Not that you cannot get an order from far-away places depending on your networking.

In fact, you must look for orders at construction sites or orders to supply blocks for government projects.

Only be sure of payment.

The block-making machine is constructed locally and the Lister engine to drive it is in all cities. You will also need pallets constructed by carpenters.

Normally, owning a tipper lorry makes the job easier and more profitable, but that may be too much for a starter.

As your business improves, you will get one.

Blocks are not easily stolen, and prices are about the same in the same locality.

Therefore, there is no price war and you can calculate your profit ahead.

With about N250, 000 one can take off, that is assuming you are leasing the land. Ultimately, you will need to have your own land.

This is a reason those in this business find it easy to own houses.

They think ahead and buy land in anticipation of future business.

Before their present location gets tight, they acquire land in a virgin area at usually ridiculously low prices.

When the place is being opened up, they are the first set of people you see. Water is important.

If you are not where water is readily available, you must factor the cost of water into your price.

The skill you will get from the labor you hire. It is not impossible for a labor team to work for different block makers.

It is an open business, no secret recipe. Your block and marketing will stand you out.

MARKETING. Locate in a conspicuous place and be friendly to the bricklayers.

Give them some returns to recommend your blocks to their principals. It is no bribe; it is a sales promotion.

CAVEAT. Never cut corners. If you make 40 blocks from a bag that is to give you 35, it will affect the quality.

Be nice to your labor hands, they can also get orders for you. Replace blocks that are broken between your office and the site.

It is not the buyers' fault. Usually, you add extra to take care of this.

12. Book Keeping.

Book-keeping is the sole of accounting which itself is the sole of business, and yet many organizations and rich individuals do not do it.

What most people do is make sales, take cash to the bank, withdraw, and make more purchases, and make more sales.

They do not separate costs to expose the leaks. Many stores do not even have stock cards. I wonder how they survive.

What you do is once, or twice your man calls to post the books. If the organization's business is large enough, you may need to station a clerk there permanently.

This business does not need much money to take off. The most important thing is the skill. Like all things, if you do not have, you can purchase.

Take tutelage or hire an experienced person and learn as you practise.

You do not need any licence to practice and you do not even need to be an accounting graduate.

As a matter of fact, most people doing bookkeeping in companies are not accountants.

Mostly, they are school certificate holders or old WASC people who have refused to develop themselves.

Definitely, an office and an impressive one is paramount, not as much for work as for prestige.

Your potential clients are merchants, small businesses without accounts section such as schools, pure water concerns, printing presses. Your market is enormous.

The greatest challenge you may have is to convince them of what they stand to gain. This should not be difficult.

First, they will see the business more clearly; they can see what profit they are making and see leaks to block.
Their Banks will like it and respect them for it. If they need the bank's help the bank will insist on proper bookkeeping.

Frequently, you will hear statements like "that is how our fathers have been doing it". Tell them things have changed and give examples of his contemporaries who are into it.

Charge reasonably, and for this, you can ask those already on the field. The accounting stationery they will buy through you, which is another source of revenue.

Therefore, if you live in Ibadan, try them at Gbagi and Aleshinloye, those in Kano talk to them at Fege Market, Aba people, see them at Ariara market.

Talk to the small companies too, pure water people. It will amaze you that many of them do not keep records.

MARKETING. This is not a business of handbill distribution or posters. Introduce your outfit on your cute letterhead with well-crafted English.

Do not write an epistle, they will throw it away and please deliver by hand.

What your outfit does, what your customers will gain, and who is behind the outfit will suffice.

Follow up with a personal visit, not reminders. This is personal service, your presence is important.

Please dress like a finance man.

Put on a white or blue shirt and a tie.

CAVEAT. Do not crook books. Show your client the actual picture.

13. Brain Box Repairing.

New cars these days have brain boxes and they are expensive to replace. However, what many motorists do not know is that they are repairable.

The mechanics collect huge money from you and repair the old one.

This biz came to my knowledge by chance when I was researching this book and I took the chance.

The interesting thing about it is that it is simple to repair.

All you need is a meter to read the connections on the board inside the box, as there is nothing inside the box more than an electronic board.

A sound radio technician should be able to repair it easily and quicker than those repairing it now.

Unfortunately, the radio repairers do not know a thing about this. For sure, electronics and physics graduates should not find this difficult.

Get friendly with a radio mechanic and practise with a damaged brain box and you are there.

Do not tell me it is impossible. Japan today bosses the entire world in electronics, which they copied from the UK by using the same system.

Carpenters open up whole upholstery set to copy. Now, having done that, polish it up with education.

Good and neat workshop, with all workers wearing overall. Make it look big and people will accept it so.

You now visit mechanics and vehicle electrical technicians (rewires) telling them about your set up.

Give referrals a cut of the money you make and before you know it; you have more than you can cope with.

MARKETING. A fine quality biz card is necessary. Personal contacts with car electrical technicians and mechanics supported with superb performance are all you need with your signboard.

You may take some time on the air to promote yourself as a recent arrival and one in town. What is your business name? Let it sound like this.

CHUKS ENGINEERING.
(Japan Trained Brain Box Engineers.)

CAVEAT. Never repair in the presence of customers. If you do, you undervalue your work and expose the secret.

If they did not do it in my presence, I would not have known how easy it is to repair and you would not be reading this.

14. Radio And TV Programme Presenting.

With due respect, many of these people owning private programs on the Radio are not graduates.

If they are doing well for themselves as they are doing without higher education, how will those with degrees fare?

And you know what, believe me, it does not take much. You just have to know how to talk and many people can talk.

Take some tutelage from established broadcasters to show you the ropes.

The joy is that as soon as you buy the time, usually for 13 weeks for a start, by the time you are halfway, you will get advertisers to pay you for advertising their products.

If the program is interesting, some big ones charge as much as 20K for five minutes airtime and how much do you think they pay for a minute?

Little, very little.

They can charge as much because their programs have many listeners. With persistence, you will get there.

Many stations are springing up, and so there is no problem getting slots.

You can start with a new station if the old ones are expensive.

I know a person who started with Orisun radio station at Ile-Ife because he could not afford those at Ibadan. Now he holds programs in both cities.
Strive to be original or you simulate a successful program of a station and air your own on another band but with an original title.

There are many angles not yet exploited by the current practitioners.

Look at it differently and fashion out a fresh angle to it all.

For example, they are all giving riddles that are sometimes trite and tale-telling fiction as authentic stories.

Nothing bad because listeners are enjoying it.

Bisi Olatilo reports celebrities' parties on the screen why cannot somebody start one on the radio live as you do footfall commentary. There are no more quizzes on-air, which used to enjoy wide acceptance in those days.

Why is nobody doing it?

Why don't you sell quiz competitions among secondary schools in your senatorial district to your senator?

There is no program criticizing these ailing agencies such as Water Corporation, IBEDC, and others.

There is no limit to advertisers if your program is ok.

You may even have organizations sponsoring the program. Politicians, churches, schools, traders, pure water businesses, manufacturing concerns, the list is endless.

When you are well known, broadcasting will open more streams of money for you. They will hire you as MC for both private and government and corporate parties.

Besides, you can voice adverts jingles, which may be in the tens of thousands.

On top of it all, you will be a celebrity. It does not come better than that, does it?

MARKETING. Initially, your radio station will announce your arrival.

You may lean on established broadcasters to pull you up. From that moment, you are on your own. If the program is good, it will advertise itself.

CAVEAT. Please do not make claims that are not true in the adverts you run. If you do, it will ruin your program and credibility.

Vet thoroughly the claims of adverts brought to you. There are fraudsters out there ready to sacrifice your credibility for their pecuniary interest.

15. Business Centre.

Daily, people type letters and make photocopies.

Applicants have to apply for jobs; small business people without PCs have to type letters, quotations, and proposals.

Besides, students will type projects, and professionals will have one thing or the other to do on the computer.Oh, what of commercial printers, they bring a lot of business but you must have a computer artist proficient on COREL DRAW.

Sometimes, this is handled separately from the business centre, as the operator will not have time to type letters. People do not notice, but this one spins money too.

All you need to start are a couple of PCs, a printer and a copier. It depends on how much you have.

With the erratic power supply, you need a generator set.

The capital to commit will determine your level of entrance. I must add that without a generator you are not in business.

One other thing is that you must strive to know a little about repairs; otherwise, you will be working for the technicians.

Well sited, you are on the gravy road. Site your outfit in academic areas like Universities, Polytechnics, Secretariats, both state and local, court premises, and commercial places. At this level, you will need a scanner and binders.

For commercial printers typesetting, you will need to open your shop amid printers.

For the general business centre, you may add digital photography.

MARKETING. Open a business in an open place for a start. Print pretty flyers and business cards. Leave the rest to word of mouth if your job is supper.

CAVEAT. Get an excellent operator with a sound knowledge of English.

Operators with bad English will spend one hour correcting a job that should not take over twenty minutes.

Do not be penny-wise and pound-foolish. Do not buy obsolete machines.

If you have to go for used ones buy a solid one. (With androids and powerful phones, this business is becoming less lucrative.)

16. Car Wash.

Along Akobo road in Ibadan here is a car wash charging N500 per car.

I know because I washed there before.

Besides, for this book, I have studied them. Now, what does it take you to start one like that?

If they wash 30 cars a day, that works out at N15,000.

Nine thousand naira a day is actual money and your raw material is water, which is almost free.

In some cities, people will gladly pay more.

Do not lose money; know your market inside out. I was told of a place where they charge N700 to wash a car.

The secret of this business is that you have to site your outfit along a road trafficked by those in A and B economic class.

These people can pay the charges. Study your area properly, there must be one or two places you can site your own.

If the place has not gotten a stream, or you cannot connect with the government water supply, which is not reliable anyway, dig a well. Water for washing does not need NAFDAC approval.

After this, get a water pump, some meters of hose, a couple of buckets, some washing towels and you are on.

I must add that if you want the calibre of customers to take you higher in the economic ladder, add class.

Rich people do not spend their money with people outside their class. You may not believe me, but that is the truth.

Ask Benz and big car mechanics, they do not share garages with bus artisans because rich men will not come there.

Wash the cars sparklingly clean.

Go the extra mile to please your customers.

If your customer brings his child, make sure the child drinks a bottle of mineral even if the dad declines your offer.

Next car-wash, the child will drag his father there.

Kids and women have a lot of influence on their man.

If you have the means, you may add drinks while they are waiting for their cars to be washed.

It spoils nothing.

One thing, since you are dealing with elites, two dailies will increase your value.

Even if you are not quick enough to wash their cars, paper, music, TV, and drink will keep them busy.

I do not have to tell you, you need to add hot water to wash the engines for extra income.

It is called steaming and there are machines built for this. This will come when you are financially strong.

In the beginning, make do with ordinary water.

You will also need to add waxing of the car on request for more income.

I cannot overemphasize this. In business, especially this type, there are three things, which differentiate you from others.

Class, Class, and Class.

MARKETING. Your service will advertise itself as you are already on a major road.

Even a blind man driving cannot miss a car wash. Clean well and that is all.

Add extras like waxing of the body for extra income and little vehicle maintenance advice free.

Many new car owners do not know a thing about cars and so your advice will come handy.

I have seen a car owner who did not know where to put water in the car. Yes, I have.

If you are on express roads like Ibadan /Ife road, you can take an advert on the radio. Those traveling will stop to wash and relax.

CAVEAT. Your labor hands must not have light fingers. Watch them carefully as people may leave valuables in their cars.

It does the business no good if your hands pilfer money and cassettes.

17. Catering.

This differs from the cafeteria, even though both may be combined and people do.

We are talking about the business of taking catering to the people as against people coming to the canteen to eat.

The caterers are the people that prepare food for parties, conferences, seminars, meetings, and so on.

The clientele is legion.

For example, we will always have old parents to bury, marriages to cement, houses to warm and chieftaincy titles to mark.

Consultants will hold seminars and big organizations will have meetings and parties to hold even as many of them do not serve food at their annual general meetings.

All the ceremonies mentioned earlier on will require food to be prepared and the caterers make this happen.

For now, old and married women are very common doing this job but I do not know why young graduates cannot do it.

I would prefer to give such a job to a dashing young lady or man to giving it to a grandma. By the time you are 40, you have made enough money, and you retire or move to something else.

The first requisite is that you have to know how to make a delicious meal and a variety of them too to cover a wider ground.

The equipment needed are serving plates, coolers of various sizes, and cutleries.

Your workers must be neat in their overalls, and they must be courteous while serving guests.

You will need a shop in a place trafficked by wealthy people where you exhibit your wares to let them know your trade.

Charges depend on where, when, what and who. If you are cooking for Zenith Bank, you will charge them higher than working for me for instance.

You will charge higher for two cows than one. If you are based in Lagos and you are going to work in Abuja, include the cost of accommodation and transportation. Therefore, it depends.

Liaise with others in the trade to know what is happening. You will need this association as they may contract the job to you when their hands are filled up.

In this business, you have some free food to eat and even take home; you get to know people, and then you make good money.

For labor, you use undergraduates, and junior people looking for extras.

You pay them for the parties they work not on a monthly basis except the administrative staffers.

Besides, your own children and siblings come in handy when they are around when you have them that is.

MARKETING. The best way to advertise is to prepare salivating meals.

Support this with a beautiful business card, strategic location and pretty signboard.

You may add radio ads as well when you are getting big.

Please make sure the MC gives you compliments and recognition at the party.

If there is a band-playing, let him sing some pleasant things about you. Seek friends in the right circles.

If you join a social club like your city's recreation club or army and police officers mess, it helps.

CAVEAT. Let your food arrive on time and hot. You do not want to be like the caterer for a party I attended the other day who brought food only when half the guests had gone in annoyance.

This is food, please ensure a high standard of hygiene.

If your principal says you should not take his food home, please do not and ensure your assistants do not too.

18. Church, Go and Start One.

You laugh. I know some people will want to crucify me for this, but no regrets.

My allegiance is to my readers and my conscience.

My mission is to show you ways to make money, and this is one of them. I am a Christian, but the church churns out money.

If you are endowed and trained, it is money-spinning. Since this book is about businesses you can do.

I will be remiss in my duty if I fail to include this. I do not have to mention names; you only have to go through the list of private

Universities or the list of private jet owners to understand what I am saying.

Some people do not even attend any theology school before they start.

I must say I do not subscribe to this. No matter how endowed you are, be trained, and probably serve tutelage.

I call this bag carrying for the forerunners. Carry somebody's bag before somebody carries your own.

To be honest, you cannot give what you do not have.

You can learn under an established man of God if you do not want to go to a seminary.

When you graduate, work a bit with him, ask for his blessings, and start your own.

Do spiritual consultation and confirm that God supports you. It is a tough job even for the chosen.

For every Sam Adeyemi, hundreds have fallen along the way.

However, it is two ways rewarding.

You win souls for God and win riches for yourself.

These days, you have to be very Knowledgeable to lead a flock as your members are professionals.

You have to be a pastor, an evangelist, a prophet, a councillor, a motivational speaker. All wrapped into one.

It is a tough job unless you want to swindle people and I do not have a hand in that.

The church gurus- Ajiboye, Oyedepo, Okonkwo, Abiara, Olowere, and others have come a long way, and they have paid and still pay their dues.

They are deep in Knowledge and spirit. I cannot say more.

MARKETING. Marketing a church is an extensive field.

I guess in years to come, we will have church administration in our higher institutions.

They use all tools in marketing, including free feeding.

Signboard, radio and paper adverts, cards, billboards, flyers, mobile advert all marketing tools are used.

CAVEAT. Choose an anointed man of God you fancy and follow his steps. Do not cut corners and do not expect instant rewards, as they may disappoint you.

Be faithful to your God and your sheep. When in doubt consult the number one consultant, GOD.

19. Club House.

This is an advance stage of beer parlors. You can develop your beer parlor business to club level for high net individuals.

This takes a lot of dough though but it can be done.

You make money from registration and donations from invited guests. See what   Ken Caleb Olumense, the governor is doing with clubbing in Ikeja.

If you do not know, Olumense is the owner of Nite Shift Coliseum in Ikeja. You can start small and aim at something like that. The governor did not get there in a day.

20. Comedy.

Ali Baba, Basket mouth, and the rest are out there making cool money for making people laugh.

If you have the talent to make people laugh, this is your goldmine.

You become a friend to the mighty, making real money doing what you enjoy. I told you entertainment pays, and comedy falls here.

Clear, audible voice and good command of English come handy even though you can crack your jokes in broken English or the vernaculars, depending on your audience.

In fact, if you are a polyglot it helps as it increases your versatility and therefore your market. Your customers are legion, the government, corporate citizens, and individuals.

They also utilize comedians as MCs. Comedians must be able to make jokes out of any issue. It, therefore, requires spontaneous reactions to issues to make your listeners laugh.

This shows you it is not a job for dullards.

You must have a high degree of cerebral capacity, which you call upon to make witty comments on issues.

It is more of a talent than learning because a story made funny by a natural comedian will be flat when relayed by a non-talented person.

With the talent, you can improve yourself by learning. This includes watching the masters live or on CDs.

The www (internet) is a veritable source of materials for comedians and all professions.

MARKETING. It is principally by contacts and press. If you are in the good books of the entertainment writers in the papers, they will hype you to your millions.

CAVEAT. Be original and have a unique style. When you get a chance,

21. Commodity Brokerage.

As I am writing this, there is a man somewhere looking for a D8 caterpillar to buy and there is another one having one to sell.

Find the two, connect them together, conclude the business, and take your share from both sides.

This is the biz local people call the commission agent.

There are scraps in companies, secretariats, local, state and federal, Teaching hospitals, Research institutes, Universities, etc.

This business includes things as small as typewriters to something as big as a 5000kva generator.

I know a couple of guys in this line who are illiterate Millionaires.

The problem with educated people as I said elsewhere is that it leaves many lucrative businesses to illiterates and this is one of them. Ironically, it is an educated man selling such products to the barely literate people cheap.

In almost all the places I mentioned, if an Engineer is not heading the selling team, it will be an Accountant or a Materials Manager.

There was a scrap deal some people I know made with IBEDC that fetched the least among them two million Naira after refurbishing and selling the materials.

All over the country there are scraps in IBEDC offices, water corporations, Transport companies, and so on.

More often than not, those selling either do not know the value of what they are selling or simply do not care. They come out at ridiculously low prices that buyers cannot lose.

To do well, you need connections with such organizations. Sometimes, you may have to register, but once in, it is a matter of time before you get something to buy.

To move faster in the business, Befriend auctioneers if you cannot get the licence yourself. This will give you an advantage over others.

You must have eyes and minds for this business and be passionate about it.

One deal can make you forever.

Walk with your eyes open. Often, owners of such materials and equipment have even forgotten that they are there.

You may be the one to awaken them to sell it and make money for both sides.

MARKETING. Pretty business card and contacts with a lot of leg work.

For a start, you may not need an office as you need not carry stock.

A deal may give you a pleasant office for people to visit you.

If you have a large stock, you may need to use the newspapers. When using papers, be careful you put your advert in the right place.

Adverts burn money fast if not placed appropriately and properly.

CAVEAT. Be careful. Find out the source of the product you are buying. People sell things that do not belong to them.

There was a case of people buying a long broken down earthmover, which did not belong to the supposed owners. Caveat emptor.

22. Community Newspaper.

I am surprised at the dearth of local Newspapers in Nigeria. Not that it will not sell; people are not just thinking about it.

I am aware of Oriwu news in Ikorodu but why is it that there is no (Eko Akete) in Lagos Island Why no Bodija news in Ibadan and Ekiti Kete in Ado Ekiti?

A local newspaper is a newspaper that reports a locality to the world and the world to the community.

It will concentrate its news on the happenings in the locality.

The marriages, the schools. Chieftaincy titles, sports, the local government activities, etc. in the community are reported.

It tells the community important news outside, useful to them.

For example, it would be foolhardy of the editor of such a newspaper to ignore the USA presidential election just because it is foreign news.

Where to put this in the paper however depends on the editor's judgment.

Two people can start it and use more hands as the business grows. You will need an office for advertisers to submit their copies. Initially, the paper may go for free, but adverts will defray part of the cost.

Now, do not go singing the impossibility song. Read the story of Dr. Sunny Ojeagbese, the boss of Complete Sports and Success Digest Extra. He with his wife started that empire with N6500.

Advertisers are limitless for a local newspaper because the cost of space is cheap, compared to national dailies.

Therefore, many people will afford it. In addition, because it concentrates on a small area, it suits most adverts.

Therefore, you will need to approach Schools, Churches, and Block Makers.

Hairdressers of repute, Estate Agents, Eateries, and so on. We must carry along your local government to place government adverts in your newspaper.

You notice that even National newspapers seek government patronage;

Printing is not a problem as there are local printers. It is advisable to start small and test the market,

Test the water with a foot before you put the second. More often than not, it will not start as a daily.

Start as a weekly newspaper to feel the pulse of the readers.

You will use their responses to adjust to taste.

If you have not been practicing print journalism, you will need an experienced hand as a consultant.

He may not charge you for his advice.

You may also study a running successful community newspaper to emulate and later best it.

MARKETING. Use posters, advertisements in churches, mosques to announce the paper.

Thereafter it advertises itself. Existing national newspapers will also help in announcing its birth.

CAVEAT. Be objective in your reporting, giving room for the other side to have a say. Run away from libel.

23. Computer School.

The number of Nigerians that will be computer literate will increase tremendously in the next few years.

Employers are putting pressure on workers to be computer literate and even internet literate.

Some companies have interviewed via the internet.

Employers hardly offer jobs to people who are not computer literate these days.
It has already become a statutory symbol to be computer literate.

In effect, establishing a computer training school is and will be a wonderful business in the years to come.

Your outfit has to be in an open place but does not have to be a shop. A three-bedroom flat in a busy commercial area will do.

If you have a little money, you can start with a room.
It is better if you are computer literate yourself, but if you are not, you can hire one who is.

A couple of Personal Computers will start you off.

While doing it, you can take a typesetting job, even though we do not advise combining a business centre with a computer school.

They are two unique businesses.

Your potential students are secondary school students, workers and school leavers who cannot get admission and are looking for a profession.

Charges depend on time and the depth the student wishes to go.

You can make a decent living. It is not uncommon to carry your training to companies and organizations where you train their workers.

MARKETING. Posters, handbills, and advertisements in local radio and newspaper will do.

If you train them properly, word of mouth recommendations help.

You must have a signboard in front of your place.

Assist your students to get work or to set up a typesetting centre if not a business

24. Cow Selling.

You think the only place you can buy a cow is the large market.

You are wrong! You can sell and buy outside the cow markets. Many are into it already, and there is money in it too.

Do you know why there is so much money in cow selling? You do not know, I will tell you.

The reason is, the farmers of cattle eat little meat. Our northern brothers eat little meat. It, therefore, follows that you can buy cheap and sell at killing prices.

The Yorubas must send at least ten fat cows to the grave with their late fathers or mothers.

Who cares, as long as they are paying and pay they sure do.

Get a space, go to the North, and bring the cows in.

Start with about five. If you do this business well for 3 years and you do not roll a jeep, come and thumb my nose.
You only need an insignificant place in a well-trafficked place for people to know that you sell cows.

You get grass to feed them until you sell them. Please feed them well to get good prices for them.

For a start, you can get your supply from nearby and make a little profit, but as you progress, get to the core north. Your service does not stop with selling.

Transportation to the place and the slaughtering is part of your job. You make more money and make your customer happy.

One advantage here is the elimination of the intermediaries who make the price of cows to be more than reasonable at the normal cow markets.

MARKETING. Establish on a major road and support with local radio advert.

That is all you need. Personal touches matter too, friends who will tell others about you.

Let your church members know you do it.

You will be about the only person doing it in your church anyway, so no competition.

Join your town's recreation club and let them know your business.

CAVEAT. You will need an honest friend who speaks Hausa fluently to buy cheaply. I do not know why a Hausa guy cannot move to Akure or Oshogo and make his cool millions doing this biz.

The joker is to buy well so you can sell well. Veterinary doctors from the ministry may visit you, be nice to them.

As you are in the town, maintain a high level of hygiene so as not to pollute the area as this may bring acrimony.

A Veterinary consultant is necessary.

25 .Crèche.

There are career women looking for a place to put their kids while they are away at work.

Some businesspersons too would be glad to have a place to put theirs.

They want a place that is neat and safe.

A place where they will drop their kids and be sure they would meet them well and hearty. A crèche is an answer.

You can provide that service, especially if you are a woman. You only need a well-ventilated room for a start, a couple of mattresses, cots, and beddings.

You will also need some toys. You will do well to put tiles on the floor and mop the floor always, knowing that kids play on the floor.

Children like pictures, so I advise you to put a TV and DVD there where you can play children's rhymes. You also need a first aid box.

With time, you will need to register with the government. All the above is not enough to make you succeed, you must love children and their tantrums.

If you use hands, as you will do, they must love children.
If you radiate love to the kids, the parents will appreciate you and present you with gifts besides the fees.

There are examples of huge schools today, which started as a crèche. This business, like school business, is lucrative.

You do not need any raw materials and you are not so much affected by electricity.
Things can be predetermined which makes planning easy.

MARKETING. Have a beautifully printed handbill displaying merry children at a crèche and distribute them in your locality.

Please do not use European children many lazy printers lift from the computer.

They annoy me. Instead, take the trouble to take your own photograph of African children, if you cannot get such children in the PC.

You will know which houses your likely customers are living in.

From your price, which you must have fixed through research and the quality of service you are providing, you will know those who can afford your price.

Some people cannot afford to pay as little as N3000 per term, so do not waste your fliers.

There is no need to flog a dead horse.

Now, follow up with house-to-house visits and invite them to come and see the place.

While in their houses, be friendly with the kids, especially the ones you are targeting.

CAVEAT. You are dealing with kids who cannot talk.

Do not provide food of any kind except biscuits and pure water.

Do not mix up their food, do not give A's food to B. Take any sick pupil to the hospital.

No self-medication by you, except the medicine brought by the parents.

Some people use oral tranquilizers to put troublesome children to sleep, DO NOT DO IT.

26. Cybercafé.

I situate my office in a shopping complex of about 100 office rooms.

There is no other computer in the complex apart from mine and therefore there cannot be an internet connection for anybody else in the complex apart from me.

I can even say further that there is no other computer literate person in the complex.

You do not believe me. Pick any ten persons at random, eight of them cannot browse the internet but browse they must as the www virus spreads.

Where do they go? The cybercafé.

Most organizations, WASC, NECO. JAMB. PCE, the blue ships, government, etc. now do business on the internet.

It forces people to visit the cafes, and the café owners are smiling to the bank.

There is one cybercafé near my house, teenagers queue to browse at N150 per hour and how much does it cost an hour?

I tell you, not much, in fact, much less than N50.

Therefore, if you want to, this is the time to join the train.

Some couple of PCs, connected to a network, a Lister Generator, some PC tables, and a shop as an office and you are on.

Your shop must be on a major road and accessible by road.

If you can get yourself a place in a Polytechnic or University campus or directly in front of either, there is no way you can lose.

You just connect with any service providers and pay as you go. It is advisable to research the performance of the different service providers to choose the one that performs best in your area.

One thing though, you must know computers and love computers.

With this business, you can really be rich,

If you properly monitor and control it. If you are not knowledgeable enough about it, please learn.

You cannot leave a business to people when you do not know about it. The control will be nil, tantamount to failure before you start.

MARKETING. It is self-advertising.

Just make sure your computers are ok and not those that take an eternity to boot.

Your assistants must be good at solving slight problems that may arise.

CAVEAT. Do not allow pornography. Disallow internet rats to prevent EFCC from sealing up your outfit.

With android phones no, this may no more be profitable.

27. Daily Contribution Collector.

As I write, I have a brother working for a woman in this business and she pays him N60, 000 per month.

If she pays that out, you can imagine how much she gets at the end of the month.

I must add that I cannot partake in this contribution thing to save as I prefer going to the bank, but my detesting it does not change the reality.

People do it and there is a large volume of money involved.

Excellent business, you see.

You take 3.3% of the contribution i.e. the first contribution of the 30 days in a month. If he contributes only once and no more, you take the only contribution. Business cannot be better than that.

Do you know some people contribute as much as N1000 per day and of course some as little as N50?

To do this business, you need credibility, the ability to pay promptly, and a cheerful disposition.

Add to these, a biro, a register, a bag, printed cards where you mark their contributions, and a bike if you are so disposed.

Your customers are artisans, traders, and petty businesspeople. Do not be fooled, these people move a large volume of money daily.

The advantage of this business to you is enormous.

Besides the direct commission, you can use the money during the month.

You can also lend the money to other people during the month on interest, but be careful.

The business also affords you the opportunity of knowing many people.

MARKETING. Word of mouth is the best.

Set some people in motion to talk nicely about you. When you have started, build on the reputation.

Use handbills and business cards. Pay promptly.

CAVEAT. Be honest with people's funds.

Be careful with it too. There are boys around who may want to steal the money off you.

Collect the money and go straight to the bank.

There is a temptation to expand and why not?

But be careful. There was one here some years back that was expanding seriously after huge radio promotion, but the quality of the human resources could not cope.

They killed the dream. They collected money and did not remit to the office.

With the computer and present communication level in the country, it should not be difficult to build a fool proof control system.

28.

Debt Collection.

People will always owe money. Some people and organizations have sizable sums of money owed to them.

Because they are busy running their businesses, they cannot collect the debts.

Some companies even have a debt collection department, but since they are in the company, they cannot get much done.

The debt collector can really be very effective because he works on debt collection all the time.

Debt collection is his core business.

Like bank reconciliation, they pay on a commission of the debt collected. If you help collect 1 Million, at 10% commission, your cut is N100,000 and it could be higher depending on negotiation.

To do this, be well-read, as you may have to deal with accountants and lawyers on the other side.

Knowledge of accountancy and law may not be out of place, but superb communication skill is necessary.

You will need an office that is properly furnished in a suitable location.

You must dress well and present your organization as a professional one.

If you are not a lawyer, you will need to collaborate with one.

I am not sure there is a controlling body yet; I am aware there is a place in Lagos where they train people for debt collection.

It is a green field, which is bound to expand.

MARKETING. Personal selling, cute letterheads, and business cards. Introduce your outfit on the letterhead and follow up.

You must state those you have helped to recover debts. See Bank reconciliation.

CAVEAT. It may tempt you to use roughnecks to recover some debts as some would not pay unless threatened.

Be careful though as a rule of law is on.

Besides, it appears the law is on the side of the debtors.

See how banks are finding it difficult to recover their money even when they are secured with collaterals.

But then, handled properly, you will make your money.

29. Directories Printing.

Often I shudder at what is wrong with us.

At Heathrow Airport and all international airports, you see A to Z of London or that of the city.

You see directories of all sorts.

You can survive without asking questions.

Do we have any directory in Lagos on even Abuja?

It is so bad; our government does not even know how many police officers there are.

Nobody can tell how many hotels are and how many schools are and where.

Directories will sell any day with a wild margin. You sell advert space and sell the directories too. It is very easy to do.

Let us say you want to do directory on private schools in your state, you will need the education ministry's approval with the consent of the school proprietors association.

Hold the approval, attend their meeting, and sell the idea to them. Henceforth, visit them in their schools. The moment one registers, you are on.

Just tell them so and so has registered and the list will increase. Because they are in competition, no one wants to be left out. But let us be honest, who does not need publicity?

However, you must be good at your costing.

The cost of photographs, transportation, plates, and printing to arrive at a price per page to give you a comfortable margin.

Those who paid to print the directories will have their copies free.

Now we have spoken about the school directory. What is happening to that hospital? Who is working on hotels?

Who is working on these at the national level? Surely, the market is vast and fertile.

The joy of it is that their deposits will finance the project.

MARKETING. Good rapport with your customers and presentation of your outfit as a professional one and not one doing it because he has nothing to do but one doing it because it is the only thing he wants to do.

Do a lot of legwork.

CAVEAT. Be careful with money.
There is the tendency to spend the money as they are paid not remembering that you will pay for printing.

Talking about printing, make sure you get a good printer.

Let an outside person proofread the work.

Let individual owners approve the proof before you go to the press.

It does you no credit to have a pile of unclaimed directories

30. Disc Jockey (DJ).

Nigerians must celebrate one thing or the other.

New arrivals are lavishly christened, houses are warmed and you have graduation and burial ceremonies of dead ones.

When bands are not invited, the DJ is the next option.

Some DJs today even sing praises of celebrant for spraying. It did not use to be like that, but they have accepted the idea.

The first requisite is that you must have a flair for this job. A shy person cannot do it.

To set up, you will need an amplifier, a set of big speakers, a playing tape, some microphones, and a generator set in case they cut the electricity supply.

Some DJs even have over two speakers to the extent that when they set up, you would think a musician is playing.

One played at a party I attended with a set-up like a celebrated musician. He had about four standing microphones and the quality of the music coming out was top of the drawer type.

He even had two dancers, and he himself was not left out. I was not surprised to see the guy driving away in the morning in a Benz.

The guy has done what I preach always; he has added a class to commercial DJ.

What you charge of course depends on what you are offering and where. A DJ producing a mono sound that is hardly audible cannot charge as the one belting out a top-quality stereo sound.

It is normal to add food and drinks separately from the charges. One advantage of this business is that you will know people and with time, you become a celebrity.

Femi Otedola's daughter is a DJ. She performed during Buhari's inauguration.

MARKETING. You will need business cards and contacts. To quicken your journey you may need managers and promoters who will get outings for you on commission.

Treat these people well. When you get a chance, seize it and perform brilliantly for word-of-mouth recommendation, which is the best form of promotion.

CAVEAT. Arrive on time for functions and do not double deal.

31. Dry Cleaning.

My son did his NYSC in Bauchi state.

Returning to Ibadan, he could not get a dry cleaner to meet his standard, meaning there is a gap to fill by superb dry-cleaning service.

Not only my son, I, am tired of my current cleaner. I am stuck with him because I do not have an alternative.

Again, meaning there is a gap. Even at that, this current dry cleaner, with his shoddy service, rolls a neat Honda car.

You can stand up, fill this gap, and make your money. There are many state capitals where only big hotels provide dry cleaning services.

Bauchi Township for one was like that until an NYSC graduate picked up the challenge. A Yoruba boy, he is giving the two top hotels a run for their money. Not only that, but he is also doing well for himself.

As I am writing, in Ibadan it is N200 for a set of top and trousers for colored fabrics, white goes for N250, and suits are much more.

Now dry-cleaning is not cloth washing. Learn it.

There are different treatments for different fabrics and you have to learn about stain removal.

You may start without washing machines but you surely need industrial pressing irons and tables, washing bowls and space to dry the clothes. For superb service, a generator is essential.

MARKETING. As for marketing, use handbills and personal selling. Local press and radio will help. Old enough readers will remember Washerman at Ikeja and their press slogan in those days. "No wonder they keep coming back".

That advert series was superb and will work any day.

Take the service to your customers by collecting their clothes from the offices and homes and deliver them when due. Your labour is cheap.

Strong young school leavers can wash and press for you. Remuneration can be per piece or on a monthly basis. It depends on you and the situation in your area.

CAVEAT; The Security and safety of the clothes are important. Do not mix up clothes, always tag them.

 Appear cute, sick men do not teach health therapy. A dirty man cannot propagate dry-cleaning.

32. Engine Oil Distribution.

You say what; I say Engine oil retailing or bulk-breaking. I know of over ten young Turks in Ibadan here under 35 years in this business living in their own houses.

You only need to site in a suitable location like garages, and busy bus stops.

Do not tell me they take the spaces up, look hard you will get or squeeze yourself into a place.

 For retailing, the association will give you the measures, which you have to pay for, besides the registration fees.

In addition, get a drum or two. Since the commercial drivers are your main customers.

I do not have to tell you to be nice to them.

If you are close to them, their officials will find a place for you inside the park. The joy is that you need little capital to start.

The bulking is where the big money is.

The retailers will come to buy from you to break bulk.

For this, you need more money, as you will now have to get a tank and get engine oil in enormous quantities.

I must add that from experience and research, a good number of the engine oil sold by these people is substandard.

This arises from the preparations as some of their producers cut the corner to make more profit.

As the drivers cannot decipher the difference, producing better quality at a higher price will put you in a difficult competitive position. So play along.

MARKETING. Open at bus stops and parks and the drivers will come. Get the best quality available to sell and be nice to your customers.

CAVEAT. Do not remix as some people do. With time, your customers will know and desert you.

The drivers can even beat you up

33. Engine Sleeving And Crankshaft Turning.

I am aware this business may need a couple of millions to start but I know equally that some graduates have parents who can start them off with two to three million if only the parents can be convinced of the viability of the business and the seriousness of the person.

As I am writing this, to cut a car's crankshaft in the city of Ibadan costs N5000 and to sleeve a block of Engine, you will cough out N15,000. No reduction, it is like Coca Cola; they fix the price. I forgot to add that bigger engines attract higher prices.

Now, to think you can cut 20 shafts a day and sleeve 10 blocks, anyone in this business is a potential millionaire.

As long as vehicles use shafts and people cannot abandon worn engines for a fresh one every time they are worn out, this business will thrive. Even in Europe, they still cut shafts. I am so sure of the money-spinning.

The potential of this business that it will pay back the capital and interest within a year even if it started with a loan.

You do not open up people's abdomen if you have not spent years in medical school. You cannot optimize this business if you do not know how to operate the machine.

You do not have to be the major operator, but you have to know how to operate it. If you do not know the practical details, you will lose money, and control and management become difficult, as workers will take advantage of you. So learn.

MARKETING. The first thing here is that your outfit must do a perfect job. People will run away if you cut shafts, and they do not run well with the metals.

Your 010 must be 010, no packing, or fixing after cutting. The same must apply to the engine blocks too.

This done, mechanics will beat a path to your place.

You will have to be nice to the mechanics and be prepared to give them a commission.

This token does not kill business, rather it helps it. Before you know it, they have passed the news around.

You do not need to spend money on ads initially; all you need is contacting some established vehicle mechanics promising them their commission.

However, if you find yourself amid competition, you may need to have some radio commercials and community newspapers where there is one.

CAVEAT. The location has to be on a road that is motorable because they will bring the shafts and blocks in vehicles.

When you are starting, you must prepare yourself to buy an experienced hand.

Two advantages, one, his expertise, and two, he will bring with him some customer.

34. Environmental Engineering.

This is "big" grammar for rubbish clearing.

Jokes apart, there is more than 1000millon kilograms of rubbish in Ibadan city alone and as far as I can see, they do not bother the government except the occasional removal of trash on the roads.

Which government in Nigeria collects rubbish from door to door, as done in Europe?

As people cannot live with stench emanating from the rubbish, and they cannot remove it themselves, those involved in removing them have to be well paid. In this city, I know young men doing very well for themselves in this business.

To start, you do not need more than the operational fund for a month. This includes the cost of hiring trucks (tippers) and the cost of labour.

Usually, your customers pay at the end of the month. You are paid according to the number of drums carried.

You pay the tipper per trip and the labour on a daily basis. Of course, you will have to provide your labour with overalls (preferably white) gloves and boots.

This will add class to your set- up and earn you more respect.

You may also need to provide black polythene bags for your customers to pre-pack the refuse.

It makes your job easier as your men will just be throwing the bags into the truck. Alternatively or in addition, you provide drums.

Your customer pays for both and you make some cuts.

All this job involves is picking up the refuse dump in the truck, and tip-off at government-designated sites.

In Ibadan, you may have to register with the government.

Prices differ from town to town.

Find out what is operating in your area if you are interested.

Almost everybody, every building is your potential customer.

You, however, must understand some people cannot afford to pay, so do not waste your time with them.

Strike your deals in estates, well-developed areas, and not slums.

Watch out, some valuables may be in the trash, it is yours or your assistants to convert to money.

Remember some people make a living retrieving things from rubbish heaps.

You will do well to add sewage tank clearing with this business, they complement one another and it is profitable.

MARKETING: Print cute flyers, distribute in houses, and follow up with personal visits.

Liaise with environmental inspectors, they will recommend you to people and organizations.

Present your organization as a professional set up and behave it. Your business card and fliers may look like this.

CLEAN UP (Environmental Engineers)
We evacuate trash and rubbish from your environment at a reasonable cost.
Phone no and address.

CAVEAT: Clean properly and do not leave bits and bits here and there.

Cover the truck and do not litter the road as you move the refuse. It is unfair to suffocate people with the stench of rubbish they were not responsible for.

35. Estate Management:

A friend of mine brokered the land for one of Mr. Biggs's sites and bought 'tokunbo' Pathfinder from that single deal.

There is money in this business and the joy is that it is not regulated yet.

Estate management does not end with assisting people to get accommodation or offices.

It includes the acquisition and selling of land and buildings.

This business is a double-edged sword that cuts both ways. You will make your cut from both sides.

Usually, you get a 10% commission from the owner and about another 5% from the buyer.

You also make money from registration and transport fees.

All you need is an office in an open place and a signboard where people can see it while passing.
Please make your office neat and presentable. If I want to transact a million naira business with somebody, I would want to assess the person and this includes his office.

For now, estate management is not yet regulated like law and medicine. However, with the boom, it will not be long before the

Sur
veyors, both quantity and land coupled with the Estate management graduates cartel it.

Get in now when it is easy. There is never a dearth of customers as people are always looking for accommodation and offices.

Nigerians abroad are looking for properties to buy; corporate organizations are expanding and would always need properties in commercial areas. Individuals want the land to build houses or for buildings to buy outright.

One money spanning aspect of this business is to buy uncompleted buildings, finish them, and sell them.

You can make over 100% profit but you will need a handsome amount of money to do this.

MARKETING. Properly located office, cute business cards, and excellent service will propel the business.

CAVEAT. Be honest. Do not sell a plot of land to two people. Do not do as some who collect money and refuse to deliver to their principal.

Please try to add this to whatever job you are doing now. Use the internet.

36. Executive Bread Distribution.

Elsewhere in this book, I said some people make money from bread distribution,

There used to be a man coming from Lagos to collect bread from Ibadan, repack and sell in Victoria Island, Lagos.

That was then, but these days' people act as distributors to UAC and Leventis bread. They bring the bread from Lagos to sell in Ibadan.

To be an executive distributor is to drop the bread in the doorsteps of the wealthy and this you may add to your bread shop or kiosk. It is a job you can do very early in the morning in an area habited by rich people.

For example, if you live at Omolayo Estate in Ibadan you can distribute high-class bread in your area. The idea is to take it to them instead of them coming to you and they will gladly pay for the extra.

You will know outright that you have to be mobile to do this. A bike will do for a start, but a car with space at the back is better.

You ensure that the bread you are distributing is of prime quality because you are dealing with high net people.

You cannot collect money as you deliver to save time and cover more ground, so an arrangement has to be made to pay weekly.

Your baker will have to be carried along, or you buy outright. You will need a tabulated form for each house where you record as you deliver.

The people you are selling to cannot owe. It is easier to deal with the rich.

MARKETING. Introduce your outfit on a pretty letterhead and follow up personally. Present yourself respectfully as an outfit offering a service.

CAVEAT. Do not disappoint. If for any reason you cannot deliver the next morning let them know the evening before.

It will be frustrating to wait for bread that will not come.

37. Executive Car Hire.

Elsewhere in this book, we have spoken about transportation. Executive car hire is a special branch of transport services.

You find them at airports, hotels, and some exclusive places.

They are to serve high net individuals and well-heeled companies by moving their managers about.

This business vomits money like a faulty gaming machine.

You charge per day or distance depending on circumstances but whichever way it is; you are winning.

Rates differ from town to town.

Find out what is operating in your place. The executive you are driving may not even leave his hotel, meaning no fuel cost.

You are happy, your company customer is happy because their officer is happy being waited upon.

The cars have to be neat and in excellent condition.

If your vehicle breaks down frequently, you will be out of business before you realize it.

You can pool together five such cars if you do not have the means to walk alone.

Having done that, register your presence by introducing your outfit to prospective customers or by erecting a big signboard.

Do not forget to put car hire boards on the vehicles.

As some users may want to pass as the owners of such cars when on hire, you may not need to brand them.

Even if you have one car you can start by contracting jobs to

owners of equally well-running cars.

At the extreme, I do not see how two young graduates cannot pool resources together to get one and I am sure companies will readily extend patronage to them.

Having gotten the cars, get in contact with corporate citizens who may need your service.

With phones, they will contact you when your service is needed.

It helps to be acquainted with the geography of the country and this you get from experience and asking questions

MARKETING. Site in suitable locations where those passing by can notice you. Compact car hire. You must place signposts on your neatly parked cars.

Be friendly with the Transport or Protocol Officers of companies you deal with.

Give them calls regularly in the African way to say hello. Dress neatly and executively.

Cars must be neat and moderately perfumed. Keep records of your customers. They are not poor men, and you may need them. This relationship is part of your reward.

CAVEAT. Drive carefully, especially on roads new to you. Return valuables forgotten in your car.

38. Executive Clothing.

I told you rich men do not have time, but they have money. Clothe them and be rich.

Bankers do not know a thing about buying. I tell you; they buy an N1000 shirt for N3000. Most of the time, it is the price they buy, not the stuff. I know because I have them around me.

I know one who will not wear a shirt lower than N10,000.

It doesn't matter to him if it is only worth N2000. We should not blame them though, as they do not have time.

It is not only the bankers who dress well, so get into the blue ships and clothes their executives too.

All you need do is to have a supply of exclusive stuff that will not be seen all over the place.

You will also do well to get the designer stuff such as St Michael, Gucci, Van Heusen, for them, and add your own margin. Right from your home, you can service your clients.

As you grow, you may have a shop.

By then you will do two businesses, a boutique, and mobile executive clothier. Please, do not have to limit yourself to clothes.

You are clothing them if you sell shoes, belts, ties, cufflinks, and even pants.

It will not be wise to combine both lines, so concentrate on either the male or female line.

If the materials are not readily available in your place, you can travel to Lagos to get the stuff.

You must be sure the extra cost is passable to your customers.

This business has the advantage of little capital outlay. No shop and little overhead.

MARKETING: This is more of personal selling. You need to dress well.

CAVEAT: They will buy on credit, you cannot escape this but you can be sure they will pay because they are well paid and have the integrity to protect.

I do not advise you to sell to lower levels of civil servants, as you will struggle to collect your money.

I do not wish to offend anybody, but that is the result of my findings.

The credit sale part of this business has to be watched carefully; otherwise, you will end up a loser.

Secondly, you must look dandy. If you want to clothe me, I would want to see what you are putting on but do not overdo it.

Please do not restrict this to bankers alone.

Some companies pay more than the banks e.g. communication service providers.

I am repeating this because those I know in this trade concentrate only on bank workers as if others do not exist.

39. Exotic Dogs Rearing.

Yes, you heard me right, dog rearing for security and not for slaughter.

Even the rich are into this. We are talking about the Rottweilers, Bulldogs, Alsatians, Collies, Boxers, Labrador, Golden Retrievers, and the rest of them.

No robber will dare enter a compound with two ferocious Alsatians. No, they dare not. Increasingly, rich Nigerians are entrusting their security into the hands of God and Dogs.

Dogs are the most loyal of animals, more loyal than men are. If a dog is unhappy with you he lets you know immediately, and you cannot bribe him.

When Chief Bola Ige was murdered in Ibadan, he had over six security men. They all went to eat simultaneously.

Dogs do not do that. The man who will kill you will give you the biggest smile.

Besides using dogs for security, Nigerians are getting used to them as pets. Now, do you know a Bulldog puppy can go for as high as N40,000?

You do not believe me? Next time you see youthful men holding puppies for sale on elite roads, ask them for the price of one.

If you are in love with dogs and I don't see why not, this is a business for you. You build their Kennels with blocks joined to the fence.

Build two or three for a start and I do not have to tell you the kennels have to be ventilated. For a start, do not buy a male. For a fee, cross the females from an unimpeachable source where they have a robust male.

The saying that your piglets are as good as the boar is true of dogs too. When they procreate and you have enough money, you can then get a male from far away.

Dogs of the same parentage must not cross.

If they do, the offspring will not be strong and they may all die. The agriculturists call this inbreeding.

Now, if six dogs procreate for you 5 puppies each that is 30 puppies and at N40,000. You get N1.20m. If this is not money, I do not know what is.

Remember, dogs eat what men eat. You must arrange for a veterinary doctor to visit them now and then.

Actually, I will advise you to get your seed through the vet or the one he recommends.

MARKETING. Sell through forums or vets or fellow dog breeders.

CAVEAT. You must ensure you buy healthy dogs for your seed stock.

As a beginner, you will need the help of experienced people.

Another thing is that you must feed them well to get a good result.

Do not forget this, inseminate them for rabies and keep strangers out of reach and these include your siblings not familiar with them.

Hounds are never friendly with those who do not feed them. Keep them in their kennels in the day and let them out when everybody is in.

First thing in the morning, send them back into their kennels.

Some people only feed them in the day but this may not apply to crossed female dogs. I cannot say this too much, like all new ventures, get a mentor.

40. Fast Food.

I agree that the title of this book is businesses you can do but I am afraid, this is one business that I will have to tell you to stay off if you do not have the necessary capital and expertise.

To Nigerians, if it is not Mr. Biggs, It is not Mr.Biggs. If it is not Tantalizer, it is not.

Nigerians will not take a step lower than the standard set by these forerunners.

I am saying this because the temptation is there to say you want to try this business with a couple of millions thinking having tasty rice and meat pie in an air-conditioned place at a lower price will bring the customers.

No, it will not. I know because I have had my fingers burnt once in this business and I know at least three others who suffered the same fate.

We all thought the same way. Do something for those at the lower level and have a slice. It does not work out like that.

If you can raise enough capital and an excellent team with delicious recipes, there is no limit to where you can get.

That is why the new entrants with enough financial muscles are having their slice.

I must tell you this; UAC is there today mainly because Mr. Biggs is doing very well. (These days UAC is downplaying the Mr. Biggs brand by calling their joints UAC food court just because the child is overshadowing the father.)

This business is about having a unique distinctive taste, the money for the equipment, and the key staff.

For the workers, do what is called executive poaching.

This is using those already in the business. There is nothing wrong with this; they do everywhere it, every day, especially in journalism.

Having gotten all this, get an excellent location. It is not by accident that you see Mr. Biggs in those conspicuous places; it is by design.

Similarly, others joining them there are for strategic reasons.

So you can be sure that if Tantalizer is doing well in a place, within 24 months or thereabout you will see Mr. Biggs and vice versa

A common practice in the trade is to employ the services of a consultant to start you up. I must warn again, this is not a business for two or three million Naira because to get an excellent location can take twice as much.

It should not be confused with the snack bar business. It is a market for those at the top of the economic ladder. No compromise.

MARKETING: No advertisement for a start. Well sited, a blind man cannot miss it.

On opening day give free snacks to early arrivals.

Staffers have to be very courteous to customers. People cannot make their money under stress and expect them to spend it under stress.

No matter how good a staffer is, if found to be rude to customers, he should be shown the door, except you, can use such a person where he will not serve customers directly.

CAVEAT: Do not try to serve yesterday food by any means. Do not laugh; it has happened in one of the big one's outlets before.

41 Film House.

We are not talking here of standard film houses as the Silverbirds.

Rather, we are talking about those minor film houses where local films are shown for small fees, depending on the locality.

Every Monday, the film producers release films in large numbers, so much that you cannot keep up.

Not to miss out. The young ones go to these film houses to watch the current films.

Either you rent an enormous hall or you make a wooden structure and benches. Buy a big TV and a CD, have a connection with a video club to lend you films.

The best is to have a Video shop of your own so that you can pick the films, as you need them. The video club will be another source of income too.

Because of the electricity situation, you will need a generator.

You will need to join their association in your locality, as there is a way this association settles the copyright problem with the actors and the producers, otherwise, the police will trouble you.

Location is very important. It will not work in the cities unless in the slums or where young children are, especially those not going to school. Places like the spare parts market like Owode in Lagos.

MARKETING. With current films, the boys will spread the news.

CAVEAT: Do not allow drugs and cannabis.

42. Fishery.

We need a lot of protein. The protein from beef and present fish supply is not enough. This explains the reason we still import fish.

The question is why we are not farming fish large enough to feed our 150 million mouths and the rest of Africa.

The market for fish is mighty. Good enough, no religion is against it and it is sweet. And the sweetest, the business is very profitable.

I have to warn that you do not rush into it. Done properly, it will fetch you lots of money but done the wrong way it can send you back to your village.

To start, take tutelage or employ one who knows about it.

There are two ways to fish farming. The domestic type may not fetch much, but the percentage profit is encouraging.

Here, depending on fund, you can build tanks or do the recycling system, which brings the fish to table weight earlier than other systems.

The other is real commercial farming where you have to dredge ponds.

There are ponds as big as 100 meters by 60 meters.

You say I am exaggerating.

Ok, go to Ona- Ofun Ona-Orun farm owned by Chief Francis Olulade Mogaji in Efon Alaaye, Ekiti State, you will see bigger ponds.

Apart from getting the fish to table weight to sell, you can sell at the fingerlings stage or juvenile stage, This reduces your risk, and it reduces your profit.

Fish sells throughout the year and when you have water running through your farm throughout the year, you are ok.

This is the reason you have to have your commercial farm near a river, which you can damn.

Be sure people around you will allow you to dam the river before you commit money. You say you do not have the money, but then you can rent a pond. Search, you shall get.

MARKETING. The women will come to you.

You may take adverts in the papers and radio, especially if you have hatchery for fingerlings. You can supply directly to Hotels.

CAVEAT. There are bumps in fish farming and I will tell you some. One minor error and the result is Nil, yes zero.

Get your fingerlings from a reliable source and transport them professionally.

You can lose 1 million fingerlings if you transport them hot. Test the water for PH and chemicals.

Your water must neither be too basic nor acidic.

Minerals and metals should be in the right proportions. Remember, fishes cannot talk; the only talking they do is to respond to food or float dead.

Besides, the water must be free of predators in and out of it. The most dangerous time is when they are developing to juveniles.

Fish eat fish, you know. In one instance, 10,000 fingerlings produced 130 enormous fishes. What do you think happened to the rest? The big ones ate them up.

SOLUTION — sort and sort and sort always.

People can harvest your fish in night, so be watchful, and be friendly.

One litter of DDT in a static pond can do much havoc.

Remember again, fishes do not talk and so cannot cry.

Before I go, during the rains, keep people on the farm. If your pond overflows, you may lose all, I mean it, all your fishes.

Fishery is a course at the University, so there is not much we can do here, talk to practitioners, and learn.

Do not jump. If you follow the rules, you will definitely smile.

43. Fish And Chips Shop.

You will excuse me as I am importing this straight from Europe.

I have included it because I am aware potato chips are already in the country and if we have those here, nothing stops us from having fish and chips outlets.

Fish is already available.

All you need is a fryer and show glasses if you want to make it executive.

Otherwise, you can fry the local way at the back and bring to serve them in the shop.

This is a market for the middle class. You must also understand that it thrives more in the night and will do even better in a place where you have a high concentration of beer joints.

People drinking into empty stomachs will have it handy while still drinking or when going home as take-away.

MARKETING. Not much noise as long as you get the recipe right and your last product is tasty.

You must open in an open place where cars can pack and pick their orders. You may add chicken if your clientele want it.

Now, please do not give your outfit a village name like rise and shine or something like that. Get exotic and enticing.

Be creative, something like Domino Chips or Refreshers, the chips people.

CAVEAT. It is served hot.

The only difference between here and the big eateries is that you only specialize in chips.

Give them all the conveniences you can afford, you can always transfer the cost to them.

44. Food:

Let me tell you about the four businesses that will always bring money... Food. Education, Entertainment, and Transportation (FEET).

People have to eat and many are lazy to cook and many do not have time.

See the tons of money Mr. Biggs, Tantalizers, and others are making. What of the 'mama pu't you patronize?

 Do not be fooled, she makes cool money, real cool money.

You can start small but please and please, your food has to be tasty. I know a graduate in this business riding a car after 3 years of opening a shop.

He does not take his car to his canteen.

I also know a woman who was driven by hunger to Lagos from Ibadan. In Lagos, we introduced her to this business.

Selling for only three hours from 6 pm to 9 pm, she now owns a plot of land in Lagos. How many years?

Just two.

Do not let them fool you, food sellers make money. Now you are educated. Get involved and do it better.

Make a delicious dish.

If you cannot, forget it or hire expert hands, and make tasty food you do not have to be a female. Men can be excellent cooks as a good deal of food competitions have confirmed.

Your fund will determine your level of entry. For a graduate, I will expect you to start with a shop in a busy place. University or Polytechnic campus, Court and registry premises, Motor parks, Markets and so on.

When you search, the situation of the place will tell you if it is ok or not. With a shop, get some tables and chairs to sit, maybe eight or ten people at a time.

Freeze your water with ice blocks if you cannot afford a fridge. Even with a fridge, you may still need ice blocks when IBEDC people do their thing.

You will also need a gas cooker or a big stove, serving plates and cutleries.

The price you charge will depend on the people you serve, what you serve them, and how you serve them. Study your competitors and do things differently and better.

Give people what they want. You must buy your raw food cheaply to make a good profit. Butchers can sell on credit for you to pay in the evenings or the next day.

With good management, you cannot fail, and feeding for you and your kids is like free but not free, as you have paid for it.

I will advise you, specialize if there are many general food sellers in your area.

Porridge, for instance, sells well, but few people make it. Good and rich pounded yam will sell any day.

The problem is that people cannot take the trouble to do it well.

I remember when I was in Zaria, Kaduna State, I used to travel from Samaru to Sabongari to eat Pounded yam and the distance is over 10 kilometers. People will always go for excellent products.

MARKETING: In this business, location is very important. Have a signboard in front of your shop, Neat workers with neat overalls. Courteous service is important.

When your customers enter, ask after their families and business. Say your goodbye cheerfully and mean it. Make all your customers feel important.

CAVEAT: Do not compromise high degree of hygiene because this is food going into the stomach. Get your materials for the soup fresh.

45. Foodstuff Transportation:

I have to deal with this separately from transportation because people tend to think transportation stops with commuting people and thereby neglecting a veritable source of money making.

The experience of a person close to me also accounts for part of the reason to deal with this separately.

A motor mechanic was not doing so well in his trade but he had a fairly good truck he packs.

I advised him to use the truck in the mornings before coming to his workshop to move foodstuff from the market.

He made so well for himself that he had abandoned bolts and nuts and spanners.

You cannot blame him, with two trucks; he goes home with about N8000 a day as long as Bodija market opens.
People are making really good money in this business.

People have to eat and the food has to be brought from the major markets before they are broken down.

Have you not seen those rickety vehicles loaded to the hilt in the mornings?

Do not be fooled, those people make good money. Making N5000 a day is not uncommon and they make with two or three trips.

You may think they are dirty but when they pay their children's' fees, the School Principal does not see the dirt.

As for me, I prefer it to sweeping roads in Europe, after all, this is my country.

Well, to get in, you will need a truck, a drivers licence and registration with the driver union in your market of interest.

To perform well, you will need to understand the geography of the town. If you are not so good yet, you will learn with time.

Be patient with the women, they will show you the road until you become a master.

MARKETING. Let your vehicle be neat all the time. Dress well and be humble to the women and officials on the road.

You will stand out and it will show in the volume of business you get.

CAVEAT: Drive with care and make sure your vehicle's papers are ok. Do not mix business with pleasure, as you will be dealing with women.

Do not look for your meat where you are getting your bread.

46. Football/Game House.

Some months back, I was in my country home with friends.

But I had a minor problem—where to watch the next day's match between Arsenal and Liverpool.

I did not have to bother, said a 9-year-old friend, as there was a football house in town.

At a quarter to one on that Saturday, the hall was filled up. Although I did not count, there was no way we could have been less than 100 heads.

At N50 per head, that was a cool N5000 for the operator, and businesses do not come better than that.

All over the country, people are raking in money showing the premier league and the joy is that the matches are so fixed that you have matches to show throughout the year.

That is when you add the European cup and country internationals. You only need a couple of TVs, a cable subscription, some wooden benches, and a generator set and you are on.

If you do not have a place, get a bold-off made of wood on an unused plot of land, or use a sizable room in the school close to you. This may not make you a millionaire, but it can easily fetch you about N50,000 a month.

If you replicate it in about three places, then you are talking about good money.

What I notice is that even people with cable in their houses come to pay and watch because of the football atmosphere they get with the crowd.

For example, last Sunday, at least three cable owners, including myself, watched Liverpool and Chelsea in our local football house. That Sunday, we were more than a hundred.

I am sure if another one springs up, both will still make a handsome profit.

You know what; the person running the place also has a paid job and many jobless ones came shouting themselves hoarse.

Do not tell me they cannot afford it because fathers who could fund such projects ten times over sire many of them. Talk of resourcefulness.

You can add a football gaming machine for the young ones to pay and play. Start with one each of PS1 and PS 2.

MARKETING. Do not bother yourself, football is self-advertising. Let the environment be clean with comfortable benches with big posters of the big four-Arsenal, Manchester United,

Liverpool and Chelsea, Add Barcelona, and Madrid.

It does not hurt. If you set this up for elites, you can use plastic chairs and even air conditioners. They will pay for it.

CAVEAT. Strictly no smoking. Standby generator must be ok. As soon as IBEDC does their thing, start your generator set.

Do not open the game room during school hours; otherwise, the police will visit you. If you have to open, please ensure that school children are not allowed

47. Football School.

Yes, a football school. Boys and girls will pay you to teach them the rudiments of football.

I am not talking of the football academy that will gulp millions.

To do this you yourself must have been trained in the art.

You do not necessarily have to be a good footballer to be its good teacher. Mourinho, the former boss of the Blues, now in Italy with Roma, is not known to have been a good footballer but he has established himself as a good coach.

You will also need equally capable assistants to teach physical education and different parts of football. Make it for those aged seven to fifteen.
They will have to be graded according to their ages.

Use the premises of a government school in your area. You will use their classrooms for the theory and their field for the practical.

The football we play in this country is natural and not text-book football. Were we to add the theoretical part early enough, the whites will not be able to stop us.

 All premiership clubs have youth clubs and there are football academies.

Those kids playing football on open plots do many things wrong and if only somebody puts them right, they would be better.

I was a good footballer in those days but there was nowhere somebody taught me how to kick the ball.

Nobody told me the effect of kicking with the inside of the foot and the outside.

Nobody told me the kind of exercise to do and the food to eat.

With schools like this, we will get there. As this business will compete for time with the students' education, you will have to make do with the evenings and Saturdays.

As I always advise, add class to anything you are doing. Let them take registration forms, which they will have to pay for.

You must get a way to fence off those who are not fee-paying and who would want to take free lessons.

MARKETING. See   Judo/boxing. Go to schools and run adverts on local radio and newspapers.

CAVEAT. Their health is very important, do not overdo it. Those with bad health conditions should stay away.

You may not be able to do medical examinations for all, have it done one way or the other for those you suspect. Good luck.

48. French Language.

Start a French-language school; they will surprise you at the turnout. Let me tell you a story.

Apart from the government French schools, I never thought there are private French schools until I ran into a guy at a joint.

Circumstances made us sit on the same table, and we started talking. He told me he was good in French and that he learned it for six months. To confirm, I asked him the French word for fish, which a friend recently told me.

He promptly told me. Later, I asked him to make sentences in French, which he did.

Ask me where he learned French of all places, Iwo road, Ibadan, and I did not even know.
They write many products' literature in French, drugs, electronics, and so on. Add to this the fact that all our neighbors in Nigerian are French-speaking.

Therefore, to speak French is an enormous advantage for you in those places.

It is even said that French is the next most widely spoken language after English.

To do this business, be proficient in the language or hire a person who can teach it.

Get a place, probably a room in a suitable location for a start. You will need a TV, a CD player, and CDs;

When you progress, you may need earphones and other gadgets you have in language labs

.MARKETING: Run advert on the local radio and local newspaper, Also use handbills and posters. Charge reasonably and this you can do by learning from existing schools,

If there is none in the city you want to serve, seek advice from outside. As attention is turning to China, teaching Chinese may not be a terrible idea.

CAVEAT. Deliver properly. Meet the target set for the students.

49. Fumigation:

The World Health Organisation says all buildings housing people must be fumigated at least once a quarter, meaning at least four times a year.

Now, if this were to be enforced you can imagine the volume of business fumigation of buildings is.

Even as it is not enforced, there is still money to be made.

For sure, all eateries have to be fumigated, so also are Hotels, Guest House, Hospitals, Schools. Companies and so on.

I tell you; you do not need any special skills.

Get the necessary chemicals, mix them at the right proportions, get a spraying pump, an overall, a protective goggle and a glove, you are on.

Come to think of it, the chemicals are cheap.

Yes, they are cheap, and that is the secret of this job. For a deal running to N100, 000, you may not spend more than N15,000 on chemicals and labour.

People do not understand it, they think you are performing miracles and people respect miracles.

This business is an elite business, so you prospect for customers in a place populated by well to do people.

If you are connected enough to land retainership with big companies and organizations you have made it.

Imagine, if you are the one fumigating UBA branches in your region.

You and their managers will be on the same economic level I tell you. Some people have their roofs being eaten off by termites, add them to your list and you will smile.

MARKETING: Personal contacts are important for big jobs. Print business cards and use steel plates on IBEDC poles and walls with a message like this;

FIRST CLASS FUMIGATORS
phone number and address.

You may even start without an office. You can also use radio and local newspapers for adverts.

CAVEAT: When fumigating, think about the people.

Do not overload and allow enough ventilation before you allow the people in. Fumigation is best done for companies during the weekends and for households when they are all out.

Remember, whatever kills a rat will kill a man if inhaled or swallowed in large enough quantities. Now you say what is he saying?

You only have to look at how much your legislators are going to spend on generators in 2020 to understand what I am saying.

One is that there is no solution to electricity problems in the near future and two, generator business will continue

50. Generator Sets.

I am not saying you open a shop. No, to compete with the established traders on this directly may not be wise.

They are the masters. But you can play safe by staying in the middle.

For example, brokerage generators sale to cooperatives by connecting them to the importer.

You should get a good price this way.

The members pay, and the importer delivers, and he gives you your cut. It involves no capital of yours except the travelling expenses.

If you sell N20, 000 Tiger generators to about 200 members and you make N500 on each one, that is N100, 000 and it could be more. This business is for groups of people with fund.

They may not pay at once, but as soon as they complete payment, they deliver their sets to them.

Look, this is the political era and politicians can do anything from unbelievable to ridiculous.

You can talk to your local government Chairman to buy generator sets for all teachers so as to encourage them to teach well and improve the standard of education.

He will do it because teachers not only man the polling booths, they also man the minds of the people.

If he does not buy for the teachers, he can buy for the chiefs and elders. On orders like this, you can easily net N1000 per set.

MARKETING. Personal contacts and social media.

CAVEAT. Deliver as promised and always build a safety valve for your commission. People could be smart, you know.

51. Grind Rice:

If Nigerians in England eat ground rice, I do not see any reason they are not eating it in Nigeria.

I tell you grind rice is sweet. Quick to prepare, it will be the darling of bachelors and up and mobile executives.
The technology is the same that makes yam flour. It is a matter of grinding and sieving.

Rice may be difficult to grind but if they grind it in London, they can grind it here.

The problem I envisage is that the price per Kg may be higher than that of semovita but then it is grind rice and the difference is there. It is in a class of its own.

One needs to identify the market and sell it to it. It is not impossible to distribute it through supermarkets.

Alternatively, you can distribute using a vehicle supported by loudspeakers.

Like special bread, you can start by concentrating in an area inhabited by those you know can afford it.

For example, if you live in a place like Bodija in Ibadan or Gowon estate in Lagos, you can produce and concentrate your product there.

Even if you do not stay there you can produce from outside and bring your product there. Source of rice, which is the raw material, should be considered seriously, as fluctuations in supply will affect production.

You can liaise with local farmers in rice-producing areas to stabilize supply.

Since this is food, you will have to get NAFDAC approval with time. This should not be a problem if you maintain a high standard of hygiene.

MARKETING. There are various ways as discussed. Your situation will decide what and how of the marketing.

One thing you cannot compromise is the packaging. It has to be beautiful and durable.

CAVEAT. Maintain a high standard of hygiene. Separate the stones and dirt from the rice before grinding.

52. GSM Accessories.

Many people are making good money from selling handset accessories.

The secret of this business is that the margins on the products are very high, as high as 200%.

I will give you an example.

I once bought a desktop charger for N200. This same charger was bought by my son for N150 and N250 by another person.

Now, all three sellers made a profit. You can imagine the percentage of profit made by the man who sold at N250.

Like stationery, because the cost is little, the profit margin is wide and buyers mind little. What is N50 anyway to most people? That is the secret of this business.

They can establish if you are in a well-trafficked area like Iwo road in Ibadan, Ketu in Lagos, Agric Bus stop in Ikorodu, Central Market in Kaduna, you will make good money.

The source of the materials you are selling is important. To sell well, buy well. Apart from chargers, items you can sell include batteries, pouches, cases, screens, and so on.

Please differentiate your business and do not forget that this business differs from the selling of GSM sets discussed elsewhere in this book.

To minimize mistakes and quicken your journey to success, take a few weeks tutelage.

MARKETING: Establish in a place where you cannot be missed and be nice to your customers.

If they return an item for reason of malfunctioning, change it immediately. He will come back and so will his friends.

CAVEAT: Source properly. If you bought an item of N50 for N70, you have made a 40% error. It is worse than somebody who bought the N2000 item for N2200

53. Guest House:

The guesthouse business is hoteling without the noise that goes with it.

They are meant for people who need quietude. Couples who want to get away from the noise and relax or businesspersons who want to get away from it all, to recover lost vigour.

They are smaller than, never as big as the Sheratons. Small buildings in serene areas devoid of noise. You charge per night and or hourly basis. You must provide food, snacks, and drinks too.

From the above, know that we do not mean this for this and that set of people. Your service must be top of the shelf kind and you must be good at it.

And you may charge higher than hotels of the same standard, as you are not likely going to make much from drinks.

The irony in Nigeria is that both practitioners and users do not even know and recognize the difference between Hotels and Guesthouses.

It is you, the promoter, who will establish and enforce the difference.

Do this and your customers will come. Please read Hoteling and subtract the hullabaloo, you get a guesthouse.

Since we do not have many Religious rest houses yet, clergies prefer Guesthouses. Serene Sites are better for guesthouses. Like hotels, you will need a licence.

54. GSM Phone/Handsets.

Apart from fuel and gas, I do not know of any SME business that has built more comfortable people than Handsets selling in the last 7years or so. Look around you, you will see examples.

There is a guy here who bought two tokunbo cars at a total value of N2.5m in a day and 5 years ago, before he veered into this business he was nobody.

If you still doubt me, have a visit to the Computer Village in Lagos or drive round the commercial areas and see how many GSM sets shops.

People buy handsets for many reasons. Many change theirs regularly because they believe it is a statutory symbol.

Many are so careless like me they lose it and buy twice in a year.

Because communication technology changes with different functions for sets, and this is rapid, people want sets that move with time. What we are saying is that the market will always be there.

You will need your shop in a commercial area. Do not choke yourself up in a blind corner and think the customers will come. Stay in the thick of the battle.

When people want to buy, they will go to where they have more choices, besides you will enjoy what economists call internal economies of scale.

The source of the purchase of your products is important. You must have solid agreement on how to deal with faulty sets, guarantee, and margins. Remember, buy well to sell well. Support your products with a guarantee.

MARKETING. Have your set-up in an open place in a commercial area. Do promotions supported with radio advert. People like cheap things.

 Besides, people do not seem to know there is not much difference between N2, 850 and N3000. It is a marketing gimmick, use it.

 If a promo like that pushes 1000 sets out of your outlet in a week, you cannot complain. Be nice to your customers. Rude attendants should not have a second chance.

CAVEAT. Do not sell second hand or used GSM sets as some people do unless you have identified them to your customers. Here, he knows what he is buying.

You cannot fool people for long. It does not make excellent business sense to mix used products business with fresh ones. Integrity is very important and pays in the long run.

Faulty sets within the guarantee period should be replaced or repaired immediately.

55. Handwriting Teaching.

One problem facing primary and secondary school education is handwriting. People will pay you to make their children handwriting beautiful and legible.

Look around you. Except for children going to special schools, children's handwriting is horrible. The reason is this, schools do not teach writing again.

Where they do, they do not do enough of it. I must, however, tell you you need a special skill to teach people how to write well. If you do not have the skill, hire someone who does.

Remember, you need not be a doctor to set up a hospital. You yourself can train yourself through the internet and train your workers.

You will not set up to compete with schools but to complement them. This means your set up will function in the evenings and weekends. For a start, one or two rooms with tables and chairs will do.

You may also need to send your workers to the students' houses if they so desire, which is of course at special charges. What you charge depends on where and how. You must charge enough to give you profit and maintain the business;

MARKETING: You will need handbills and advert plates on walls and electricity poles. Caption…

IMPROVE YOUR CHILDREN HANDWRITING TALK TO US,
THE HANDWRITING PROFESSORS…
0802231A441

Please note that handwriting experts interpret a person's personality from his handwriting, they do not teach handwriting.

CAVEAT. Deliver as promised.

56. Alternative Medicine.

This is a multimillion Naira business. Herbal is the future of medicine in the world.

See what the Chinese are doing with alternative medicine.

I am not sure Yem-Kem went to the university, see what he has done with herbal medicine and there are hosts of others there.

All you need is one sure therapy for a disease.

Until tomorrow, an excellent one for Malaria will sell. So also will an effective one for pile.

Next time you have a bus ride, take time to look at the neck and top back of people, you discover that about 30% of them have eczema.

They will be glad to cure it and have smooth skin. A simple recipe of readily available materials will cure this totally.

You do not need any machines, just mixing in your bathroom and you are there.

There are many products you can research on and make to solve people's health problems.

If you do not inherit it and you cannot go back to your village, take tutelage from people in the trade.

You are not an herbalist; you are an alternative medicine practitioner.

You learn it as you study medicine.
Call yourself a doctor, the police will not arrest you.

Choice is an herbal product for malaria.

It started in Ikorodu. Now I have seen their salespeople in Ibadan, which is evidence of magnificent times.

Imagine you have a cure for diabetes, high blood pressure or AIDS, you are on the way to being a millionaire.

And I can tell you, there are African cures for the first two and with enough support, there will be a cure for the third one.

Do not start going about NAFDAC. Start first but make sure your product is efficient. Start in a small area and when accepted, you can then expand.

Those who have used your products will spread the news with word-of-mouth recommendation, which is the best form of promotion.

A vehicle, preferably, a branded compact car will help the business but if you do not have, get a kiosk in a well-trafficked place.

Support this with a megaphone, especially when human traffic is high.

The herbal medicine I use for piles is not NAFDAC registered, and I have been using it for upwards of two years and it sure works which is what is important to me.

Maybe this story will inspire you, because I know average Nigerians look for reasons why a thing will not work, not reasons it will work.

Besides, many of us are sitting on acres of diamond without realizing it.

My PA has a friend whose father is an Alfa who treats people for ailments. Naturally, the friend had picked up some cures from his father.

After NYSC, as wont with many, he could not get a job.

Now, it so happened that one of his friend's fiancé visited and in the morning, the bed sheet was full of semen.

Apparently, the girl's system was not holding the sperm, she was suffering from what the Yorubas call 'eda' and with this ailment, and she will never be pregnant.

Ok, the problem had become open, so it had to be discussed by the friends during which time the Alfa's son assured them of a cure using what he learned from his father.
Like magic, the preparation was applied and that same month the girl got pregnant. It was the end of trauma for the girl and the beginning of a flourishing business for my PA's friend.

The guy had been looking for a job when he actually should be employing people. Many are like that.

MARKETING: When you are growing, you cannot do without Radio and Press advertisements. Initially, make do with a megaphone, mobile adverts, and direct sales.

You should know that exquisite packaging is inevitable. You can go to offices and markets etc

CAVEAT. Make sure your product performs the functions you claim and prepare it hygienically.

57. Re Purchase And Financing.

Every day, people get profitable jobs they cannot service for lack of funds.

With a reasonable amount set aside, you can fill this gap and make some money.

For now, you do not need a licence to perform, as long as you have the fund. If you have a powerful person in the finance sector, he can assist in the funding as long as the intention is not to defraud.

This is how it works. You have a presentable office in a commercial place preferably not far from the banks.

Let people know you finance projects by advertising. You do this through your signboard and flyers.

Before you know it, people will flock your place. People are always short of funds as the banks are not forthcoming. Please do not get me wrong. You are not a moneylender but a financier. You monitor and control the spending.

For example, the borrower walks into your office with an LPO to finance.

He completes the documentation, which he gets to do with money anyway. You confirm the originality of the instrument.

Write the issuing house to domicile the payment to your account as you are financing it.

If the borrower does not like this, drop it like a hot potato. If he agrees, finance the LPO and deliver.

When payment is made into your account, pay him the agreed portion of the profit. It is as neat as that.

Even at that, the borrower must put down some collateral. You must be careful of LPOs that have large margins.
They may be traps to borrow money not to pay back.
Companies like MTN or Guinness will not give LPO with margins that will kill the company.

You may have some links in the bank around to send referrals to you when people do not meet their requirements. Do not overtrade.

Play it safe and do not use your entire portfolio at a time.

Give room for shock-absorbing.

The agreement between you and the borrower must be drawn up by a lawyer so having a lawyer as a partner or friend will not hurt.

MARKETING: Respectable office in an open place. Smart flyers and word-of-mouth recommendation. You may add press advert and radio adverts with time.

You can loan to salary earners and deduct from the source.

CAVEAT: Do not be greedy. Research projects properly before you commit funds. As careful as banks are, they still make mistakes.

Be very careful about the financing of government jobs.

If you ask me, I will say stay off but if you are sure of payment, you may go ahead.

Never ever, bend the rule to domicile payment. That is your last line.

58. Honey Distribution.

In this book, I try to point out that distribution is a separate business from production.

The same thing is applicable here. Honey distribution differs from the production. Specialisation is what the economists call it.

There is a lady doing this business, and she is not doing badly.

She gets her source from Benue state where she did her youth service but Benue is by far not the only source of genuine honey.

From Igbeti in Oyo state, you will get genuine honey. Just get the genuine honey and sell it to the rich and hospitals.

Honey is medicinal and all of us need a tablespoon every morning.

Please make sure they do not adulterate it, otherwise, you will compound people's health problems.

Get to the farmers and buy directly from the source. Let me tell you simple tests for pure honey. It does not attract ants.

It does not wet paper. If you put it on paper, it stays and does not spread. Insert a matchstick and strike the match, it must ignite. If they have mixed it with water, it will not ignite.

Even if it stays for ages, it does not solidify.

About every person is a potential customer. Convince them of the medicinal value and they will buy. I must confess that not everybody can afford pure honey at about N1000 per litre.

So do not waste your time talking to those in the D group of the economic ladder. As much as they need it, they cannot afford it and there is nothing anybody can do about that.

Take your sample to health organizations and offices, especially those above 40 years.

These are the people who need it more and those who are likely to be in the earning bracket to afford it.

If you press properly, you may convince companies to buy for their executives to reduce their medical bills.
This is true. If the executives use it daily, they will see the difference it makes on their health. I know because I use it.

Now, this should tell you something that you have to know honey and its uses properly before you can do well in selling it.

A guy has written a book on the uses of honey going for about N1000. You may need to get this and digest it.

It will help you with your marketing. In any case, marketers will tell you, you cannot market a product you do not know. Product knowledge is the first and the most important thing about a product you want to sell.

You have to know your product as you do your spouse if not more. I am now in possession of a report on 50 uses of honey. If you need it, I will send it to you free through e-mail.

MARKETING. Take advert in newspapers as you can sell by post using plastic bottles.

Personal selling is equally important. If you have an. office, support it with radio advert. Package professionally.

People buy both the back and the inside. Get what I mean?

CAVEAT. Please do not adulterate your honey, it injures people's health. It is going to the stomach, so a high degree of hygiene is important.

59. Hostelling.

People hire houses to run a hotel, so there is no reason why you cannot hire a house to run a hostel. That is if you do not have one.

In the cities, it is becoming increasingly expensive and difficult to rent houses. In Lagos suburbs, to rent a three-bedroom flat, you may be coughing out a whopping N500, 000 for two years rent.

A single man or woman would be wise to stay in a hostel.

But where are they?

I have an engineer brother in Lagos who sleeps in the office but who would have preferred a hostel at a reasonable price.

This is a paying business that people are not thinking about. It pays in places where you have singles and students.

It may be difficult to bring strange faces together but people do not know one another when they meet in schools and become friends. Circumstances also do make people friends.

Besides, friends may approach you as a group for space.

Now, the kind of business I am talking about is not bed and breakfast, which is another business on its own.

I am talking about a situation where two, three, or four people share a small room and pay weekly, monthly quarterly, or annually as the case may be.
You must be sure of the kind of people you are taking in.

They have to complete application forms with guarantors, a letter of introduction from their places of work, and photographs.

Do not take anybody outside students and salaried workers and please verify their claims.

These two groups have a lot to lose if they misbehave or default. Please note that this is not a business for towns but mega cities where you have accommodation problems.

MARKETING. You must have a big signboard and visit nearby tertiary institutions to tell them about your hostel.

Have advert plates at strategic places, bus stops, IBEDC poles, and walls, with time you will be tired of the business.
CAPTIONS

YOUNG SHALL GROW
HOSTEL ADDRESS
PHONE NO.

OR

STOP FATTENING THE SHYLOCKS
STAY IN A HOSTEL
NAME, ADDRESS, AND PHONE NO.

CAVEAT. Be careful whom you take in.

Maintain discipline and do not allow the place to be turned into a brothel.
These must have been spelled out properly in the agreement anyway;

You will have separate hostels for each gender and please provide agreed amenities.

A regular supply of water is a must. Have all this in place and you are on. A standby generator will increase the value of service provided and therefore the price charged.

Elsewhere in this book, I have told you entertainment is money and Hoteling is part of it.

There is a demand for hotel services everywhere, even in the villages.

People will have to travel and sleep where they do not have houses.

People will have to relax after a strenuous day's job. And people will need to spend holidays away from their homes.

There are classes of a hotel, from a one-star hotel to five stars like Sheraton.

Your capital will determine your point of entry. For a starter, a fenced three-bedroom flat will do.

It does not have to be yours; you hire it. Equip it with beds and beddings, freezer, and plastic tables and chairs for drinks.

There must be tables and chairs in the room as well, but this time wooden table because your lodgers may want to write.

To move the standard up a bit, you will need to put TV sets.

A room in a city like Lagos goes for more than N3000 a night and you will still have those who come to rest and go in the afternoons paying about N500 an hour.

A room can easily bring N3000 a day. The drinks and pepper soup are additional income.

It is not uncommon for a set-up like this to net N6000 profit on a good day.

However, you must have strict control; otherwise, your workers will short charge you.

I advise you to outsource food, pepper soup, and receive a commission to concentrate on the proper business, which is lodging with drinks.

If you can comfortably combine all, better do, because there is a big margin in pepper soup.

MARKETING: Have big signboards from all the junctions leading to your hotel and minor sign posts directing customers to the place. Hotels do advertise themselves.

No matter where they are, people will come there.

You can make handbills and distribute them in the locality.

Be very nice to your customers and remember Hotels have to be neat.

Your guests need not go home with bed bugs and lies. Give presents to regulars during festivities.

CAVEAT. Please know your customers.
If you suspect anyone not to be clean, stop him politely. You do not want the police to seal up your place.

Losing two or three customers is better than police trouble. In fact, this will give a positive image to your Hotel.

Customer confidence will grow.
You must know your DPO (Divisional Police Officer). If I have a hotel, I will know my (CP) Commissioner of Police.

Fumigate regularly.

Do not forget you need a licence.

60. Hoteling:

Elsewhere in this book, I have told you entertainment is money and Hoteling is part of it.

There is a demand for hotel services everywhere, even in the villages. People will have to travel and sleep where they do not have houses.

People will have to relax after a strenuous day's job. And people will need to spend holidays away from their homes.

There are classes of hotel, from one-star hotels to five stars like Sheraton.

Your capital will determine your point of entry. For a starter, a fenced three bedroom flat will do. It does not have to be yours; you hire it.

Equip it with beds and beddings, freezer and plastic tables and chairs for drinks.

There must be tables and chairs in the room, but this time wooden table because your lodgers may want to write.

To move the standard up a bit, you will need to put TV sets.

A room in a city like Lagos goes for more than N3000 a night and you will still have those who come to rest and go in the afternoons paying about N500 an hour.

A room can easily bring N3000 a day.

The drinks and pepper soup are additional income. It is not uncommon for a set-up like this to net N6000 profit on a superb day.

However, you must have strict control; otherwise, your workers will short charge you.

I advise you out source food, pepper soup, and receive a commission to concentrate on the actual business, which is lodging with drinks.

If you can comfortably combine all, better do, because there is a big margin in pepper soup.

MARKETING: Have big signboards from all the junctions leading to your hotel and minor sign posts directing customers to the place. Hotels advertise themselves.

No matter where they are, people will come there.

You can make handbills and distribute them in the locality.

Be very nice to your customers and remember Hotels have to be neat.

Your guests need not go home with bed bugs and lies. Give presents to regulars during festivities.

CAVEAT. Please know your customers. If you suspect anyone not to be clean, stop him politely. You do not want the police to seal up your place. Losing two or three customers is better than police trouble.

In fact, this will give a positive image to your Hotel. Customer confidence will grow.

You must know your DPO (Divisional Police Officer). If I have a hotel, I will know my (CP) Commissioner of Police. Fumigate regularly. Do not forget you need a licence.

61. House Cleaning:

You will not do the cleaning on your own; you employ women to do it for you.

There are people doing this business as contractors with reputable companies, and they are doing well for themselves. They sweep and clean the offices.

They get the contract and pay the workers.

The same principle they use in providing security for companies they use in this.

You too can set up and get into the companies. Do not accept defeat.

Now, even if you cannot get a contract in big companies because you are not well connected, you can make a good living by arranging to clean the houses of rich people.

I told you, rich people are lazy, their children are even worse. Set out your outfit as a house cleaning one and employ some women to do the cleaning.

When payment is made, you take your cut. Usually, you will need to introduce your outfit professionally with a sound introductory letter followed by personal visits.

One or two households for a start and good performance, referrals will do the rest

I know what I am saying. My compound is about two plots and with all the children away, it is a hell of a job for madam (my wife) to clean up.

Consequently, we have to engage a woman to do the cleaning and we pay on a weekly basis

The idea is, you get the job, agree on the payment, and get the women to do the cleaning.

Your workers will not come on a daily basis, could be once or twice a week.

Your job could include washing of clothes, ironing of clothes and even cooking, the more the better. Charges will depend on what you do and how long it takes.

You have to charge in a way to keep you in business.

Do I need to tell you that, it is not everybody who can afford this service?

Do I also need to tell you that you must document your workers?

You must know them well and they must be guaranteed.

MARKETING: Brief and professional letter of introduction on a cute letterhead and equally cute business card followed by personal calls.

To cover wide grounds, you may employ one or two sales representatives on a commission basis or on salary.

Steel plates advertisements on walls and IBEDC poles in strategic places will assist. Let your ad run something like

GENERAL HOUSE CLEANING WE DO IT
CALL CHUKS ON PHONE NO

CAVEAT: You are going into people's houses, be careful of the people you employ so they do not put you in trouble.

Please clean very well. Performance is the word here.

62. Ice Block.

The Truth here is that if the electricity in your area is not steady; do not venture into this business.

Otherwise, it is profitable because your raw materials are water and polythene bags which costs about N2 per block.

Even if you are selling a block for N30, you will still make a profit, though your break-even date may be extended.

But where the electricity is erratic, do not touch it with the longest pole.

You will be disappointed to find out that you cannot harvest more than once a week when you should harvest about 5 times.

There is absolutely no problem with sales, especially during the dry season.

Even during the rainy season, you will still make sales but at very low prices.

Who cares, it is water anyway.

Do not be deceived by the adverts you see in the paper telling you to make N10, 000 a day.

Ask them how much investment.

You cannot run this business successfully on a generator unless you have a battery of machines and a giant generator which will not cost peanuts.

An ice block machine making 25 blocks goes for about N200,000 but some could go as high as N250,000 depending on the quality.

There are the middle women who come to pack from your plant(block making machine).

Alternatively, you can have your outlet in busy markets or motor packs. You should look for opportunities to sell to those throwing parties.

Some hotels buy to freeze their drinks too. And your big customers are beer joints. To save you trouble, sell in quantity to the resellers and keep your peace.

Remember manufacturing differs from distribution, and that is why big companies have distributors.

MARKETING. As said earlier, when sited properly, the sellers will come to you.

There was a time sellers went to Oshogbo in Osun state to buy when electricity in Ibadan was down.

Your advert!

ICE BLOCK SOLD HERE

CAVEAT. If you are going to this business, buy a machine that is solid. Usually, you ask existing iced block makers to advise you.

They will tell you a durable one.

Protect your compressors with stabilizers with a delay system. Be hygienic, as some of your customers will use the block to sell icy tea and things like that.

63. Internet Marketing.

Gigantic business. Real extensive business.

If you handle it properly, the business can make you a millionaire in a year. I predict that in another 5 years, internet marketing will be a course in our Universities and Polytechnics.

To get into this business, you have to be tutored. Attend seminars and then have a mentor. There are gurus in Nigeria and on the net.

Some of the masters in Nigeria are young men who got wise early and most of them are business sons and daughters of Dr, Sunny Obazu Ojeagbese, the boss of Success Digest Extra and Complete sports. Among them are Lateef Olajide, Henry Minor, Olatunde Samson, Akin Alabi, Iyabo Oyawale, Olakitan Wellington, and others like Kolawole Bisiriyu.

These people and others run seminars on different aspects of internet marketing and none of them is poor. Yes, the Akin Alabi in the house of representative in Abuja, was once an Internet Marketer.

For God's sake, I am not talking about those internet termites who want to reap where they did not sow.

We are talking about people marketing goods and services to the world via the internet.

In internet marketing, you can make money through affiliate marketing, blogging, web design, e- book marketing, forum building, forex trading, and a host of other means.

To partake in this big business, you may not even own a computer.

A  phone, access to a café, and browsing knowledge have adequately equipped you.

If you are desirous of making an internet marketing career, the author runs a training school.

MARKETING. You will need the newspapers and www. (World Wide Web). A computer.

CAVEAT. Do not cut corners. Take tutelage from accomplished marketer

64. Martial Arts School (Judo/Boxing School)

If you hold belts in judo, you can start a judo school in your area. Self- defence is becoming more imperative in Nigeria.

Most of your students will be teenagers made up of students, artisans and park boys.

Do not limit it to boys as girls need to learn martial arts to defend themselves from bullies.

This means you may need a lady partner.

You should encourage those with the abilities to turn professional.

They discovered Michael Tyson like this. You will need a sizable room, which may be one hall of the secondary school around you.

Things like mat will have to be provided by you initially, but practising dresses, your students must provide. In an ideal place, you need running water, but in Nigeria where do you get that? Instructors and students go home to bathe.

MARKETING. You will need flyers to be distributed at schools and parks as driving apprentices like to learn self-defence.

A signboard in front of the school or place you are using may be necessary but do not obstruct your host signpost.

You can also advertise in a local newspaper if there is one in your place.

CAVEAT. You must have a way to know the health situation of your students.

This you can do by giving them application forms to complete. The forms will be a source of revenue for you.

People with heart problems do not learn Judo or boxing.
Immature people may be vengeful, ensuring that there is no animosity between practising students.
Tight discipline is necessary because learning differs from the competition.

Even in competitions, you do not compete to kill.   Please know the nearest hospital to you, should you need them. You can combine it with boxing.

65. Junks Removal.

As I am writing this, I have junks in my yard, which will thrill me to pay to remove. In the junks is a complete exhaust system of Peugeot 504 car that I know will be worth at least N1000.

That is not all. There are bearings and some electrical materials of value, which I do not need. As I have them in my house, many houses will have them too.

And all of them are looking for people to remove them at a price so they might get fresh air.

One thing about this business is that it is a double-edged sword, which cuts both ways.

You make money for clearing the junks and you make money selling valuable items in the junks.

In many houses, there will be more valuable things than the one in this example.

Some may have serviceable TV, electronics of all kinds, upholstery, washing machine, vehicle spares, and kitchenware.

Some of these appliances, when repaired, can fetch you real money. This business can make you rich.

Handled properly, any junk remover who clears this junk in my compound cannot make less than N10,000 on top of the clearing fee.

There are houses you will get a much richer heap of junks. Such is the amount of money you can make if you set up a junk removing outfit.

If people make money from trash heaps, you should understand why junks should bring in more money.

What you charge depends on the time it takes to remove the junks, the distance, and the degree of affluence of the owner.

Yes, doctors use this system, charge them as they can afford, but do not overdo it.

You inspect the junks before you charge. This gives you the opportunity of assessing the valuables, which will influence your charges.

If you realize you will make good money from the scrap, you can come down on price. It is important you present your outfit as a professional one, out to help people remove the junks in their premises at a fee.

You should not present yourself as a lowly rated person doing the job as a survival strategy.

Present it as the only job you want to do not as the only one available to do.

Good appearance is not negotiable, supported with a cute business card and letterhead when introducing your outfit.

It must have occurred to you that you will not get much in an area inhabited by the poor.

Your target markets are estates and areas inhabited by the well to do.

By their houses and cars, you shall know them This is understandable because these are the only people who can overlook an old TV, an old set of furniture, unserviceable vehicles, old clothes and so on.

In all honesty, you are as interested in these items as the fees.

Having retrieved the materials, you sort out the valuable ones. If you are not sure of what it is, ask people before you throw money away.

Some of them you may have to tone up to fetch more money.

Clothes, you may wash and iron and furniture you may reupholster.

When you have sequestered the valuable ones, sell the rest to iron smelters through their dealers.

Remember, scraps are not rubbish.

There is no special skill necessary for this job except that you must have an eye for those things that are valuable.

A way out is to gather your junks and ask an experienced person to have a look at them.

This way, you will learn. For ease of operation and more profit, one needs a truck for scrap clearing.

If you do not have one at the beginning, you will need to hire at a negotiated price that will still leave enough margin for you.

As you cannot remove the junks alone, you will need boys to assist whom you will be paying as they work.

They do not have to be on a monthly salary. For prestige, you will need an office and of course, a phone.
Of course, I expect you to have prospectors looking for business for you and whom you will pay commission. Sources of business are estate agents, rug and tiles cleaners, and builders, and so on.

At times, you may have to point a junk to your customer because he may not even know. Pose simple questions such as sir, are you still using that, pointing at the object.

Often, you will get answers like, oh that, no use for it.

A comfortable man does not have time for small things like that. Play on that and see the reward. Of course, you will meet some that will cling to 19 years old shoes because they are strong. Learn how to deal with those. Polish their ego and gently move on.

MARKETING.   Superb stationery and the clean appearance of a professional are inevitable. Brand your truck to tell people about your business.
Have advertising plates nailed to walls and IBEDC poles in strategic places reading like,

JUNKS?
DO AWAY WITH THEM CONTACT WOLE
Or

GOT SCRAPS TO CLEAR?

CONTACT ......Do not go to areas inhabited by people on level D of the economic stratification ladder.

Do not present your outfit as one begging to survive.

Present it as a professional outfit offering a service they need. This will show in the kind of dress you wear, presentation and your office.

Your business card is an asset. Use it when you have the opportunity to be with people who may need your service. Can combine this with trash removal.

CAVEAT: Clean up properly and professionally. Do not take what you are not given. Your assistants must be closely watched.

Light-fingered ones should be sent packing, pronto.

66. Land.

I am aware this is not a business for a starter, but as you will surely be able to do this, I want to let you into the secret of wealth-building.

It is a secret of the wise old men. I know because it has paid me handsomely, and it still does.

Buy land and wait, do not wait to buy land. Some plots of land I bought for N9000 a piece in 1995 are now going for N1,500,000 apiece.

In places like Lagos or Abuja it could be more prosperous As long as you buy land genuinely, there is no way you can lose unless the government takes over all land even then they will compensate you.

There is no business that compounds money like land. Oh God, it will never depreciate or meltdown as we have with the capital market now.

Not that the stock market does not have its own advantages.

For one, it is much quicker to turn to cash.

Back to the land. If you have some sizable amount of money and you do not have time to supervise a business, buy land from a reputable agent, and keep.

Do not buy directly from landowners, they will swindle you.

Buy from registered land dealers with impeccable records. These people know the landowners and their antics.

Even among these people, there are many dubious ones. Its not so bleak, there are some excellent ones. Search for them and you will get them.

I know Lagos and Abuja are hells on earth as land speculation is concerned, but then nobody stops you from buying and keeping land in your state capital. Does everything has to be Lagos?
Having bought the land, you will need to have people around to monitor the land and these people you hand out something when you visit.

If you have the fund, you can fence it up. When you are selling, it will increase the value.

MARKETING. No big deal. When you want to sell, tell the people you bought from, they will help you to sell at a commission.

CAVEAT. As soon as you sign the papers, survey, and start pursuing the C of O. It does not guarantee there will be no troubles, but it puts you in a safer position.

67. Laundry:

You laugh.

You say washer man or what is this old man saying again.

Yes, washerman but with a difference, only this time, your hands will not even touch water, the only thing you handle is cash.

The snag though is that it will take a couple of hundreds of thousands of naira to start. By now, you know what I am getting at.

Get a couple of washing and drying machines and install them in well-populated areas and higher institutions.

The latter has the advantage of a better electricity supply, but you may have to fold your hands when they are on holiday. Perhaps you do not know that the electricity company gives preferential treatment to higher institutions.

If you do not have enough funds, you may not bother with drying machines, after all, we are in Africa where the sun shines till 6 pm.

They will wash with you and dry at home.

However, to have a complete setup, dryers are necessary.

You may need some hands to assist you, especially where water is a problem.

MARKETING. It is important you open shop in an open place very near your potential customers.

You will need a signboard, flyers, and business cards to announce your arrival. You may also have plates nailed to IBEDC poles and walls in strategic places.

MR CLEAN WASHER MAN
(We wash and dry your clothes while you wait)

OR

WAIT AND GET WASHER MAN (Wash and dry your clothes in 10 minutes)
OR
MACHINE WASH AND DRY

CAVEAT. In this business, electricity is the key factor. You must factor into your price the cost of electricity if you are generating it yourself.

Now, you can charge different prices, charging higher when you use a generator than when you use IBEDC.

Your customers will understand. As much as possible, do not keep people's clothes because they will get mixed up.
It is strictly wait-and-get.

Give attention to special and different fabrics and regulate the machines accordingly.

Clothes with running colours should not be loaded into the machine.

68. Management Consultancy.

You can be a consultant to people in your field of specialization; There are consultancy jobs in all fields.

The prerequisite is that you have to be deep in the field, you will be a consultant.

Many retirees act as consultants to their companies in their field. Those lecturing in banks training schools are mostly retired bankers, even as some of them are still working.

Usually, you will need an office where to visit you. Your office has to be properly sited, and it has to befit the status of a consultant. You do not have your office at Ajangboju in the outskirt of Ikorodu and want to service companies in VI.

They will not talk to you because you are not one of them.

You will introduce your company as suitable, using corporate letterheads and business cards.

In this business, personal contacts matter.

Those who know your competence must be able to recommend and when you have the chance, make the best of it.

One more thing, to get a Government job, they may compel you to register with management institutes such as the centre for management development (CMD), Lagos
There is a lot of money in consultancy because there is no raw material apart from your brain and stationery and you are not affected by import or export restrictions or even exchange rates.

In this business, think for the companies on how to solve their problems.

You give them a proposal and if accepted you are on.

Alternatively, they may ask you to solve a problem for them. Do not tell me it is difficult. Think hard.

The present Attorney-General gave a consultancy job to a green lawyer in the Pfizer case.

This is a guy who is barely seven months in the bar.

As said earlier, you can consult on virtually all fields of endeavour, such as Marketing, Market research, Insurance, Materials management, Personnel management, Production control, Transportation, Logistics, Security. Accounts, Credit Control, Advertisement, Sales Promotion, the list is endless.

Do not limit yourself to companies.

The government is the biggest spender, and they spend millions on consultancy.

Have you forgotten the Police equipment fund where N200M was spent on a party? It is a consultancy job.

I have handled seminars worth millions of naira with state governments.

MARKETING. Contacts, contacts, and contacts.
After this, performance.

CAVEAT. Performance is the word and make good all promises made before they give you the job.

Consultancy is a veritable source of money-making because EFCC cannot even probe it.

You cannot value knowledge. An MBA in Lagos business school costs about N20.0m and you get the same MBA at UI for much less.

You understand what I mean.

69. Manufacturing:

Jesus, there are hundreds of products you can manufacture and sell. Many of these you can do in your bathroom or backyard.

Let me tell you about manufacturing. You cannot really call yourself a very rich man if the machines are not running for you.

In buying and selling, which we call commerce, only men work for you and machines work more and faster than men do.

The day you have the machines working for you is the day you are really there.

Dangote made millions bringing in sugar, cement, and all the rest. I tell you, he did not start to make real money until he started producing, ask him, he will tell you.

Look at it this way. Most distributors for Nigerian Breweries are millionaires.

Now, if you pull their resources from distributing beer together, can it match that of NBL? No, it is not possible; the slave cannot be richer than the master.
I have gone to all this to encourage you to focus on ending up as a producer of goods. You do not have to start with a factory like Eleganza at Oregun. Start from your backyard.

You can start producing things like aftershave. Soap, Raticide, Perfume, toilet wash, polish, gum, chalk, liquid wash, ceramic cleaner, and so on.

The list is endless. Go and read the story of humble beginnings of Michelins, Guinness, and Coca Cola. Anybody born into these families today is a millionaire.

Even in Nigeria, we can talk about similar families.

Take Alabukun powder, for instance, it has endured and Okoyas and his friend Adedoyin are painstakingly building their dynasties. You too can be like them.

 If you are desirous of going into manufacturer let us talk or you talk to consultants in your field of interest

70. Mc.

I know of MCs charging as much as 25k per show.

If you have what it takes, get in. To rise quickly you will need to be on the air. Please see Radio program presenting.

71. Meat Shop.

No set of people is more class conscious than Nigerians. I want to show my neighbor that I am better off.

Add a little of class to meat selling and you are on the way.

I am used to Ibadan and I cannot say there are many meat shops even as I cannot say categorically that there is none.

What is common is selling in the markets and those hawking.

I know however that a young lady is making real money doing this business in Lagos.

For God's sake, why is this not replicated all over Lagos megacity and other sizable towns and cities in the country?

Our problem is this; we leave money-spinning jobs to not so educated people.

We call them mean jobs. For God's sake, what is demeaning for a graduate to have a meat shop?

Everybody wants a job at Mobil or Zenith, jobs that are not there. Baxter, the meat people, is a meat company in England with outlets in all their towns and cities, bringing meat nearer to the people and employing thousands in the process.

Who is doing that here?

The advantage of this business is that buyers know exactly what they are paying for a Kilogram unlike the normal meat sellers who ripped people off.

You need a shop in a place with high human traffic, a freezer, Table, Cutlass, Knife, and a table scale and you are on. I must add that you have to be neat and use overall. I always emphasise differentiation and class, this one is not different.

You may need clearance from the local government. I bet it, if I know Nigeria and Nigerians as I do, being a legitimate biz, the officials won't choke you up when you are just starting.

Did I tell you, you need a generator set?

Yes, you do, to keep the unsold fresh all the time. If you do not have one, you can keep unsold with a frozen fish dealer in your area at a price that is usually meagre.

You can also apply this system to fish and pork where permissible. I have deliberately left out chicken because its importation is banned, and I do not subscribe to illegality.

The fish dealers may refuse to store pork for you overnight. The alternative is to fry the remains and sell.

Now, you say pork, yes pork, people eat it.

I have watched people picking fried pork at Agric bus stop in Ikorodu in large numbers; they reduce a heap in a tray to nothing within minutes in the evening. If the woman is not making a profit, she would have packed up, but she is there every night.

God, the people we call illiterates have more money-making sense than we do. Let me digress.
A woman very well known to me was retrenched recently from a teaching job and I advised her to be frying yam in a well-trafficked open place if she did not consider it demeaning.

She took my advice and one month after she employed another hand. She had come to thank me.

She did not have to, I always passed along and I know business is good.

MARKETING: Open a shop in an open place and stay till about 9 pm if possible for people closing late from work.

You may do vehicle promotion in your area distributing flyers to let them know you have opened.

Plates or cloth adverts on walls and IBEDC poles in your area.

FRESH MEAT THE BEEF PEOPLE
ADDRESS
PHONE

The rest now depends on the service.

CAVEAT. Sell fresh meat; Do not force stale meat on people. If it gets bad, accept your luck and move on.

They will pay you at the end.

72. Mobile Car Care And Servicing.

Rich people are lazy, go to their homes, and service their cars for them. This may not be limited to them alone. Mobile mechanics can make money, repairing vehicles that break down on the roads.
In England, there is an AA company.

If your vehicle breaks down anywhere on the motorways, I can swear you will see them within the next 30 minutes. If they cannot fix it, they help you to the next place.

Do not tell me we have such here, because the objective of those we have here is to tow while that of the AA people is primarily to assist to fix the fault. Besides,

I am saying you can make money not only on the road but also in homes, honing up their machines on wheels.
You will have to know and love cars. Major problems you will not and cannot even handle in the homes but little ones like oil and plug change, you can do.

You can wax up the cars and even shape up the brake system. Some cars get funny overnight for no reason, such as a leaking clutch, this you can fix.

You will definitely need a vehicle for this, preferably a strong 4 wheels which you can use to tow vehicles when necessary.

Yours is a one-vehicle workshop, so all your tools must be there and of course, small items like plugs, cables, belts, filters, hoses, and so on.

You will not be of much use as a mobile mechanic if you have to travel 20 kilometres to go and buy a fan belt of N200. Think ahead and anticipate,

This business can be run alongside a motor mechanic business as customers will reach you easily on the phone. The line must be a hot one for the business only.

Well run, this business can grow to a behemoth such as AA example given above.

I am quite aware you may not be able to handle all vehicles therefore you must have contacts to refer your customers to. You have not lost anything; do not be surprised he will call you again when in such trouble.

MARKETING: Brand your truck neatly carrying your workshop address. I am not confused; a mobile mechanic must-have an address.

Put a giant spanner on top to let people know immediately that these people are mechanics.

Be in neat overalls, mechanics do not have to be so dirty. To show you are in a different class, put on accident boots.

Have business cards you give out to people and link with the national union of drivers (NURTW) in your place.

Before you know it, your phone is ringing non-stop. Introduce your service to Landlords associations of the well- to-dos.

It is a novel idea; they may want to resist the idea but press on. One or two satisfactory trials and you are on.

Remember, were it not for the tenacity of purpose and perseverance of Prophet Mohammed (peace be onto him) there would be no Islam today.

FIX IT MOBILE MECHANIC
ADDRESS PHONE
(We fix your vehicle anywhere anytime)

CAVEAT. You and your people should not tamper with people's property. Be watchful, many people still move with a large amount of money.

73. Mobile Car Wash:

As a rich man, how would you feel, if a guy bumps up in your house or office, informing you he is there to wash your car?

Now think about it.

You do not have to burn fuel to drive to the car wash and better still; you do not waste time.

You are working, doing something productive, or resting while your car is being cleaned up. It is called mobile car wash and I swear it will spin money for you.

You will need a truck and a big plastic water tank, which you put at the back of the truck. A 1000 litre tank is ok and you fill up as they deplete it.

To it you have to attach a long hose and nozzle to sprinkle the water. Please make it respectable.

Do not try this business carrying buckets to search for water.

You make it cheap and they will treat you just like that.

You need a branded truck, the tank, and your labour hands that you pay daily or monthly, depending on your agreement.

Since you are taking the service to the vehicle owners, it is rational to charge higher than others.

Watch it, do not overdo it. Charge what will make you and your customers happy.

Besides washing the cars, you can also add waxing to increase your earnings just as we recommend in a normal car wash.

In places where they have a public water supply, you can attach your hose and conserve your water.

MARKETING: You will need cute fliers and business cards which you will distribute in offices and estates populated by elites and middle class.

These are the people who can afford to pay your charges.

CHUCKS MOBILE CAR WASH ADDRESS & PHONE
We wash like new

CAVEAT. Your assistants must not be light-fingered lest they put you in trouble. Please read car wash.

74. Motivational Speaking.

They make tons of naira daily in motivational speaking, which is now the rave in town.

You need a delightful voice, ability to stand and address a crowd, excellent knowledge of the topic, contacts, and long hours of reading books.

Know a bit about everything. If you can give what it takes, it will give you fortune and fame.
You must understand from the beginning that it is not a job for the lazy ones, as you have to read and read and read, because you will address professionals who know their onions.

You only have to slip a couple of times and that is goodbye to your career.

For a one-hour speech, you may have put in over 48 hours of preparations.

Sometimes, you may have to rehearse the speech several times.

This job is a mix of oratory talent and cerebral capability. Only you can decide if you fix in.

Your English has to be impeccable. By that, I do not mean you have to be a walking oxford dictionary, but it does a motivational speaker no credit to be mentally searching for appropriate words while speaking.

You are not going to be a Bob Proctor or Zig Ziglar or Norman Vincent Peale in a day but it pays to prepare properly before you hit the road.

I advise you to understudy a successful speaker for a period. During this period he would show you the ropes, ask you to anchor, and probably handle some topics.

When you are on your own, you may initially be living on him, as he will be referring jobs to you. He will tell you and probably give you books to read.

There is no need to ride a high horse here; it will not pay you much. Soft pedal and learn from the forerunners so you do not make the mistake they have made.

.

The internet is there to assist you in your training by buying the CDs of the masters and studying them.

I do not know which books your mentor will recommend for you but I will tell you two that you cannot but read.

Books by Shakespeare and the holy book of the Christians, the Bible. The bible is full of wisdom and uplifting statements.

All situations under the sun are covered by the bible. Now and then, you will need to quote from it.

The success of this job depends first on competence and then contacts in the right places.

Motivational speakers charge in millions when working for big companies and governments. Of course, your clients are governments, government establishments, and companies.

MARKETING. Only contacts can get you the jobs.

Even when you have to give them a new idea, inform of proposals, you have to go and convince them.

Everything about you has to be corporate.

You do not go and give a speech to UBA middle management in jeans. Only the deep calls to the deep.

Use the press to hype you,

CAVEAT. You cannot over-prepare for your speeches. Rehearse and rehearse and rehearse. One gaffe and you are

75. Motorbike Stunt Entertainment.

What I see Okada riders do with their bikes baffles and thrills me at the same time. If only these talents are harnessed and organized, it could turn them into money.

Think about it. For them to be doing those amazing stunts without them being properly trained means they could do scary stunts when tutored and organized.

After all, people go to the circus and I have seen people paying to watch rams fight in this country.

Now, do not tell me it cannot be done because they have never done it before. Whenever a thought like this comes to your mind, just remember inventors like Edison.

Remember also that water had been there before Gbadamosi started bottling Ragolis in Ikorodu and somebody started packaging water in N5 sachets.

Today, you have Eva, Gossy, and hundreds of pure water outfits. Yes, it may not be easy, but then nothing happens without effort.

Gather five gifted and interested Okada people together and introduce the idea to them. Let them know they will make money and get fame.

Nobody does a thing for the sake of God, they do things because of what they will get or gain. (Put that in your head as you progress in the business.)

Start training with the help of a trained police rider and you are on.

When you are proficient enough to hit the road, hire a big place, and send your flyers and posters out.

You need a big fenced place. Where will you get that you say, I say look for it,

Musicians like King Sunny Ade and 2Face play to large audiences? Ok, go to your local radio or TV station.

They can even collaborate with you and take up the publicity.

Now, do not take on the entire country at a time. You eat an elephant in bits so start with your local government before you take your riders around.

Nigerians like entertainment and young guys doing unbelievable stunts on a Saturday evening will surely entertain.

Before the real deal, you can entertain your spectators with cultural dance and a comedian or even a magician.

You still think I am dreaming. If you do this properly in places like Lagos, Abuja, Port Harcourt, and Kano and do not make name and money, kill a dog for me I will eat it.

MARKETING. Your posters and flyers must carry a photograph of a stunning stunt to attract people. Do a rally round the area with a rider giving them tips on what to expect.

Whet their appetites and you will see how they troop to your show. Local radio and press will be of help.

You may also invite wealthy personalities to donate to increase your revenue. Research on how they organise circuses and do a similar thing.

Government approval? I do not think this is necessary for now. Go ahead, you are breaking fresh ground, the government will need you to set up regulations and control.

CAVEAT. Your riders have to be insured and make sure that your spectators are well secured to prevent accidents.

Do not allow your riders.to try stunts you have not mastered. Practise, practise and practise.

For a 20-minute musical, the musician has practised for months. No shortcut. First aid is necessary in case of an accident.

76. Music Band:

This may not be for everybody, but if you have what it takes, why not.

The first thing and the limiting factor is an arresting and sweet musical voice. Without this, with the best set of instruments, one will end a failure.

What we are saying is that a graduate of music with a good voice and necessary finance can set up a musical band. I have said it elsewhere that entertainment sells and this is one of the areas.

When Paul Dairo was going to make a choice of career between Engineering and music, his father, the music legend, I K Dairo told him, he would make more money in a night as a musician than what he would make in a year as an engineer.

Today, ask Paul Dairo, he would tell you his father was right.

There is a young man in Ilesha teaching music in one of the secondary schools whose band does not charge less than N50,000 a night during the weekends.

You must be told that to be a successful musician you have to give it all.

These days, you do not have to own the instruments.

There are musical instruments companies hiring out instruments for musicians. However, you may need a simple set to practise.

MARKETING. Personal contacts in influential circles. Cute business cards and super performance when they hire you. This is the best form of advertising.

You will also need promoters and managers to get performances for you for a cut.

Use wireless microphones and get closer to celebrants when singing.

Motivational speakers have found out that you are more effective when you are close to the audience.

The audience feels part of it, musicians cannot be different.

CAVEAT. Be prompt at occasions. Do not collect money from two people when you know you will not meet both appointments.

It is frustrating for a celebrant to wait for a musician that will not come and when you are given the chance, seize it and prove your worth.

77. Newspaper/Magazine Stand:

My vendor who runs after cars to sell confessed to me he makes at least N2,500 a day.

Now you say that is not money, but if he goes to the state ministry as a graduate, he goes home with less.

And do not forget, if he has a stand in a suitable location, he can make much more. No capital outlay.

You return unsold copies and keep your commission as high as 30% sometimes. Some even rent out magazines, but I am not recommending this.

MARKETING: The most important thing here is the location. It has to be a place trafficked by those affluent enough to buy newspapers.

You must have agile people to quickly give the papers to the prospective buyers as they drift in their vehicles.

You must be able to know which paper is bought by your individual customers to save precious time in the morning, remembering that within hours a newspaper becomes stale.

78. Non-Governmental Organisation (NGOS)

They fund NGOs in dollars. I am not talking about AIDS NGOs, that segment is saturated and no more original.

You can think of new avenues.

Commuters' Protection Association, for instance, is Ok.

What of Fuel Consumers Association? In addition, there are scores you can choose from, but you must be passionate and knowledgeable about your choice.

The NGO needs to be registered and there is always the law side of it, which may cause you collaborating with a lawyer if you are not one.

Do not be scared, you can still own one; all you need do is pay for the lawyer's fees. You however need tutelage.

Get it, it is worth it.

79. NNPC Dealership

Nigeria is opening up the oil sector, so get involved. The meaning of deregulation, which the government is trying to do, is removing the constraints and allowing more people inside.

The government will remove her hands and leave the field to market forces.

See what is happening in the GSM sector. They have created many jobs. What deregulation of the oil industry means is that more people can take part;

You can be an importer if you have the fund or join in the middle as a fuel broker.

You can even rent moribund stations and retail diesel (Ago) petrol (PMS) and Kerosene (DKO). Like gas has taken over from kero now.

One thing in this business is that you can make millions without investing a dime that is if you have the buyers.

Take Diesel or black oil, for instance, if you have a company like Cadbury taking trucks of the material from you, you need not have the cash to finance it. LPO from Cadbury, Guinness, NBL, and the likes are live orders and no bank will refuse to finance it.

Their LPOs are as good as cash.

The banks will only domicile the payment and give you your cut when payment is received.

With this deregulation, more people will retail Kerosene and while you are retailing diesel, your spouse will retail Kero.

The opportunities are limitless so get involved, the cartel is being broken.

CAVEAT: I am certain the government will put the necessary safety controls when the market is finally opened up but please let me remind you to handle fuel especially Petrol with caution and respect.

80. Office And House Medicare.

For the doctors this idea may not be novel, they call it domicile medicine.

Take medicine to houses and offices. Executives are so busy they do not have time to eat, let alone do urine tests.

Go to their offices' test and treat them for minor illness and bill them fat.

81. Organizing Excursion For Schools.

Travelling is part of education. I know mates in primary school who entered a vehicle for the first time when our school went for an excursion.

And I can confirm to you that the first and the last time I saw silos was our set excursion to the University of Ife, now OAU in 1971.

In those days, the schools organized it, but with more specialization it is being handled by agencies set up for that purpose.

This is understandable, as they will have more time to fix the excursion because it is their core business.

The way it operates is to mark out those places you want to visit. Factor in your expenses as transportation; feeding and sleeping if they will sleep and add your margin.

It is normal to give about 10% to the school. If you do not, they will not push it, so put this into consideration.

Now, let us assume you reside in Kano, you can arrange an excursion to the palace of Ado Bayero, the emir of Kano, Bagauda Lake and places of interest like that.

Those in the west can visit places like the palaces of Ooni of Ife and that of Alafin of Oyo.

You have Erin waterfalls, Ikogosi warm spring, Olumo rocks in Abeokuta, and even IITA in Ibadan.

Who says you cannot take the students to Lagos? I know schools going as far as Ghana.

And who says we cannot take children in the south to the North? The snag in this business is that you are limited to private schools because they only can afford the bill.

MARKETING: When you are set, write to the schools stating where you plan to visit and the cost.

This is a promotional letter, it has to be written in such a way as to move the reader to action.

Do not put the commission on paper, discuss with them when you visit. The school collects the money, takes their cut, and gives you yours.

CAVEAT. Do not collect people's money and run away and do not twist your nose because we have seen it done. Take excellent care, the safety of the kids is paramount.

82. Organizing Schools Quiz Competition.

You can make good money organizing quiz competitions among schools.

The better if you can get it on the air. I do not know what is happening to our system. In those days, there used to be competitions here and there, but no more.

Even inter-secondary schools football competitions called academicals are dead. God help this nation. As we were saying, you may very well be the person to wake people up from their slumber.

From the beginning, you will understand that this needs a lot of planning. You will get approval from the Local government Local Inspector Education Officer (LIE) if you want to concentrate on your local government.

If you have the means to cover the state, you will need to get the state government approval.

Now you will have to choose whether it is primary or secondary level, you are targeting.

The public schools will not participate because it involves money but there are some who will be interested and involve their students.

There are two ways to turn this into money.

Registration fees by all schools. This depends on your area. You can ask them to pay N5000 per school. This is nothing to a school they will pay. Another way is to link this with an influential politician in your area.

He will sponsor you. You can also ask for sponsorship from business concerns. I tell you, if you have a good proposal, school-loving companies can take it over.

I mean companies like those making noodles and children's food will jump at it, if well packaged as long as they know it will have a positive effect on their profit and loss account.

MARKETING. The best time to introduce things like this to a school is at the beginning of the term and the best term to do so in the second term.

Schools are more affluent then because that is the term, they pay only three months' salary. You must have a letterhead that stands out and write your proposal in good English.

Having done that, attach your letter of approval and visit the schools. Your letter for sponsorship too must be very professional.

If this project is planned and executed properly, it could be institutionalized and become an annual money-spinner that can be passed to generations.

CAVEAT. As the schools register, issue receipts and make sure you do not spend beyond the percentage earmarked for expenses.

I have seen a case where the person was just collecting the money and spending it. At the end of the day, he had overspent and could not perform.

83. Party/Events Planning.

This is another business that will be in our university curriculum in another 5 to 10 years.

People throw big parties without knowing how to manage them.

In the end, they not only dissatisfy their guests, but they also waste their money. I have seen where cars were stolen from parties and I have seen parties where food was thrown away the following morning while some guests were not fed.

A little care here and there will prevent this. For example, asking guests to park in an allocated space manned by a couple security people will forestall cars from being stolen.

Just as they hire caterers, they will need party planners who will take charge from inception to the vote-of-thanks at the end of the party. One can really make good money here.

You will handle drinks, food, travelling, chairs, canopy, etc. If you handle a funeral party for the father of a generous senator you do not need to work for a year.

I am only joking, you will need to work but you would have made good for yourself. Just remember big men do not have time but you have, use it for them, and bill them good.

MARKETING: You will need the contacts by moving in influential circles.

These are the people to get the job for you. You will need, of course, a cute business card, which you carry about with you and give to people.

Do not forget to cause the musician or MC to say some nice things about you. Finally, when you have the chance, make the best of it.

CAVEAT: Do not be tempted to run away with your principal's money, with good service you will be very happy at the end of the day.

84. Private Coaching.

There is money in education and it will be like that forever as long as we keep having children. Set up a house-to-house coaching for the children of the rich and be rich yourself.

I know a guy here who charges N15000 for Physics coaching of SS III students. But the guy is wonderful, damn good.

Once, a parent sent his son from Lagos to be coached by this man.

He is a secondary school teacher and rides two cars, one of which is a modern Benz. I am sure his salary alone does not maintain those cars.

The way to do it is to have excellent teachers, get the parents and send the teachers to them as per need. You charge them, and from this; you pay your teachers.

I have a friend who pays N20,000 a month for his 2 kids and this could be more. Now if you have a setup that handles 50 families, you are on. In gigantic cities, you can easily overshoot this.

MARKETING; You can use handbills plates on polls and walls and local radio. Your plates advert can run like something like this.

A1 PRIVATE TUTORS
PHONE NO

Do not overload walls and poll adverts, most people read them while passing and they do not have the time. Leave white space on your adverts.

85. Professional/Business Schools.

By this, I am not asking you to establish another Lagos

Business School but a school to train young people in the professions, like Accountancy, Banking, Marketing and so on. I know that young graduates can teach even those in the professional stages.

I agree that you cannot buy experience, but teaching is more art than science. Some people just know how to impart knowledge no matter their age.

So if you are in this class and especially if you are an accountant, I advise you to start one school in collaboration with some friends.

You first have to be chartered to attract students and I expect this to take a year after your NYSC at the most, believing that you would have started during your service year.

This idea allows you to finish the two parts in four diets.

That is fair enough for a serious person. And for a person who wants to train accountants, you cannot fall below this standard.

If you do not resist any paper, the better. Even if you cannot use this feat to advertise publicly, you can drop it somehow like a joke and you can be sure it will spread.

This idea can take you to impressive heights if done with all seriousness. There are examples of people who have done well for themselves through this route.

I will not mention names but in Lagos, Ibadan, Benin and even Akure, they abound.

I must add that this will not do well in small towns where there are not enough workers.

Unless the city is huge, I will suggest we limit this business to state capitals and even at that, not all of them.

You should know your area more than I should.

You do not need much capital outlay. You can use a government school because you will be holding classes in the evenings as your students are working-class people.

Make sure your first set do very well. With this, you can go to town and make noise about your achievement.

You can be sure your students will blow up your competence too. Very soon, their friends will come and you are on.

One aspect of this business I saw some guys doing many years ago. They advertised for those who had failed some papers in the final part of (ICAN) Accountancy and who was passionate about passing.

The course was for a month marathon, day and evening if you could spare the time, but the team of chartered accountants were ready.
Apparently, many had to arrange their leave to suit the time, and of course, many would just attend for two or three weeks.

The fees, I have forgotten but it was big enough and they had students.

Both sides smiled at the end of the day. I do not have to tell you that the students' number was limited and the teachers were damn good.

You can do such. I know the case-study in Marketing gives people a problem, I also know some people who passed with distinction at the first attempt.

If you are one of such, you can gather Students with this problem. If you charge 50 students at N10000 each, that is N500, 000.

MARKETING. You will need handbills to give out at offices, banks and all the places you think they might need your service. Radio advert is very important.

Let them publicize it the best way possible. These days the church can help to advertise.

Let your fees be reasonably low initially to bring many people.

When the result comes out the way you want, you can sing your song, and the more they are to sing with you the better.

CAVEAT. Do not miss the first chance. I can advise not to register unserious students for examinations through your outfit.

86. Piano/Music Training.

Come and teach me how to play piano, I will pay you. Many people do not know that with N10,000, you can get a good Tokunbo organ and plant it in their houses and play for leisure and devotions.

Train them to play the organ and sell organs to them with 100% profit. Remember, rich people do not hag much. They definitely do not have time to go to the Ladipo market in Lagos to buy organs.

This may not make you a millionaire but will definitely earn you something till you start a bigger one. But who says it cannot earn you much?

The guy who teaches music part-time in one of my schools earns N10,000 a month and I know over six schools he does that for appearing for about 4hours a week.
Do the mathematics.

MARKETING: Have a cute business card and market through churches and proprietors association.

You can cause announcements to be made for you during services and big meetings.

You can also distribute flyers at churches, conventions, and crusades.

87. Politics.

Just last week, Rotimi Amaechi, the minister for Transportation said unemployment drove him to politics.

Can't beat them, join them. Join the ruling party in your state.

I must say I do not subscribe to politics without principle but since, unlike better climes, politics is business in Nigeria, we have to treat it as such.

So if you want money, join the ruling party in your state but make sure you are known.

Let them know you. Flex muscle.

You must not be one that can be ignored.

A young man was made a fill-gap chairman in my town for about four months and before you know it, he has built houses all over the place.

I do not like it this way but since it is my mission to show you what businesses you can do, I have to tell you this is one of them.

What difference does it make anyway, whether I like it or not, the politicians are draining the soup fast, so if you do not resent it go and slug it out with them.

88. Pumpkin Farming.

Pumpkin is a special vegetable and very nutritious.

Some people even claim it has blood-replenishing capabilities that anyway is not our concern here.

We want to cultivate it and make money from it.

The difference between it and other vegetables is that you have to stake it and you also sell the fruit.
It also fetches more money than other vegetables.

During the dry season, you can make a lot of money on a plot of land. It flourishes if the water supply is adequate.

If you do not have a fund to sink a well, try to get land in a place near a river.

All you need will be a water pump. If that is too far, get some jerry cans and use your muscle.

Do not worry about the distance, if you get there to farm, buyers will come there to buy as long as it is motorable.

As written elsewhere in this book, buyers from Ibadan do go as far as Ekiti State to buy vegetables.

You may need to ward off insects if necessary. Professionals will advise you on what to use. Like vegetables, the market sellers will fight one another over your pumpkin. Just let them know where you are and they will beat a path to your place.

Price is determined by the market.

I deliberately left out arable farming because I know you need money to make it profitable but this vegetable can put food on your table.

However, if you can afford it and know the technical knowhow which you can acquire anyway, farming is a good business.

MARKETING: Word of mouth to the market women, that is all. Assist them because your success depends on their success.

CAVEAT. During the dry season, be sure of the water supply. Get your seed from practising farmers. If you buy from the open market, they may not germinate because of dehydration from overexposure to the sun

89. Ram Fattening.

This one I will show you here is not just sheep rearing but strategic ram rearing or ram fattening to be more precise.

Many people rear sheep and rams but few do it strategically, that is for a purpose and for a particular time.

The best time to sell your ram is during the Eldil- Kabir (Ileya festival). Until last year, I never knew a ram could go for as much as N80, 000.

I knew it because a friend bought. I was even told it could cost more.

The strategy is simple. Immediately after the next Eldil-Kabir (Ileya), go get the kid lambs.

Now wait, not the female but the male. Do not mix fattening with breeding.

You want to feed them for the next festival and sell. Period. The mistake many of our livestock farmers make is to mix breeding and fattening. This is not the best practice, it is always good to specialize.

Now get about 20, hopefully in your father's compound if not go do it in your village, and bring them to the city to sell.

From my research, you cannot spend more than N12000 on each and that includes the seed cost to get them to the market.

There is a young man doing this job in an enclosed place with about 50 rams.

He has been doing this job for 5 years with no other job, and he is doing fine. He cannot but do fine.

Twenty-five thousand naira profit on a ram in 50 places is more than N1m.

To me, that is a clever way of making money.

Now do not talk of no money. Discuss this with your parents, and tell them you will payback.

If you have been a wonderful chap, they will play along.

You can get their feed cheap from remnants and the bush. Since this is a job, to move around for free food should not be difficult.

MARKETING. No big deal. Ferry them to the market during the festival and you go home with your cash.

You can also make radio announcement on a station with high listeners.

Simple.

CAVEAT. You must talk to a vet. There are some drugs they give them to increase their conversion rate. Talk to the Fulani Man. Rearing these things is in their blood.

90. Raw Food Retailing.

My senior cousin owns a house in Ikorodu. He was retrenched from a teaching job because he is not a trained teacher.

Having searched for a job that was not existing to no avail, I advised him to take up selling raw food in his area. Rice and beans, to be precise.

That house in Ikorodu came to be largely from the proceeds of that business.

My mother cannot read and write but she built a 10 room one storey building from the sale of raw yam.

If she did that without formal education, what would she have done with that business with a university degree?

The Igbo man selling raw rice and beans near your house is not a stupid man, he is a rich man.

Quote me. Learn from the Ibos, the Ijesas, and Ijebus. They are the real traders. I cannot tell you more.

MARKETING: Open a shop in a well-trafficked area and stay till late. Many people buy on their way home. Be nice to your customers. Ask after the family and his work. It is a balm that soothes the soul.

91. Remedial School.

More people fail WASSCE and NECO than those with passes.

I know enough to say without any fear of contradiction that more than 80% of the candidates fail.

Only about 11% passed the just released NECO.

Now the 89% will have to retake the examinations if they want to have tertiary education.

Besides, those with passes will have to pass JAMB to gain admission to Polytechnics and Universities.
In other words, for these teenagers, there is a need to have some schooling before they gain admission.

This gap is there and the government is not doing anything about it. You go and fill this gap and make money.

I am sure you can see many of them around you. You move to a new ground and open shop.

Throughout the year they make money. I tell you how.

From January, they take students for the JAMB and O level. After this, they train people for Poly JAMB. Now as I am writing Poly Jamb results are out.

They are coaching people for Post jamb and in another couple of weeks; they will be taking in students for GCE.

Just like that, the 12 months circle is complete.

They make money throughout the year. In their own academic year, there are no holidays.

Now I do not have to tell you that they charge for registration forms and help their students to register online, which is not free.

They also help to check results as well.

MARKETING. Open shop in an open place. You can get a big room in a shopping complex and make your benches and tables.

Make nice handbills and plates on IBEDC poles and walls in strategic areas.

Look at the image which I put deliberately. Make your own better by using while boards which are neater for teachers and students and more beautiful.

EXCELLENT TUTORS ADDRESS AND PHONE
(Worst Scenario=9credits At A Sitting)

CAVEAT. Please deliver as you promise. Get excellent and dedicated teachers. I tell you, some of the NYSC members are good, damn good. Use them.

Do not be like the one my foster son attended where the English teacher should be sitting in the class as a student himself.

If your student's results are good, they will tell their friends. You can progress from remedial to full-time school.

92. School, Start one.

You see it every day everywhere. I do not have to tell you there is money in it. If you have the money go into it. You cannot lose.

There are categories of schools, so your point of entrance depends on the amount of funds you have.

Even if you have little, you can have a go at it.

There are many comprehensive schools today, which started in two rooms.

Some even started in plank bold-off

The biggest advantage of the school business is that the market is always there, you do not need any raw material and you are not much bothered by IBEDC inefficiency.

Do not mind the government; they cannot cope with the demand because they do not have the will.

Besides, we Nigerians procreate at a rate, which makes it difficult for the government to cope.

They will always make noise about this and that on education, do not mind them, start. They need you anyway.

However, when you start, give a value for the money you collect.

Get excellent teachers and use them optimally.
Usually, the lower classes may be manned by not too strong teachers but for the higher classes, you need magnificent teachers.

You do not want teachers who speak to-went English. Naturally, the pay will determine the quality of teachers, but you can strike a balance somehow between fees, salary, and teachers' quality.

Government people will come now and then, be nice to them, and as soon as you start, begin your registration process.

Even if it is not yet approved, let them know you are there. Registration in progress is better than not letting them know.

MARKETING. Unless you are rich, you cannot start with radio adverts but definitely, you will need handbills and posters in your area.

You may need to visit houses too. Churches and mosques will help in advertising you.

CAVEAT. Do not start by giving out free uniforms as some do.

People like free things but do not respect them. You do not want a school that is not respected.

Serious parents will not be looking for free uniforms as you will soon find out that those looking for free uniforms will default seriously in fees payment. Maintain your stand from the start.

They will owe you money, there are no ways around this but understand your parents and deal with them individually.
If you are leasing a house, plan to have your own structures as quickly as possible.

This is because when you make money envy will set in and the owner will drive you and set the place for his child.
Please read the crèche.

93. Sandals/Palm Sandals Manufacturing.

Have you noticed that more Nigerians are using sandals these days?

Except for the core office people, like Bankers and corporate executives, more of us are taking to the traditional sandals and the slip-ons.

Have you been to the national assembly before and see the percentage of our legislators using slip-ons?

Even during the weekends, the bankers join the rest of us.

This is understandable because of our climate.

Sandals allow for easy aeration of the feet and eliminate the nauseating foot odour associated with covered shoes in the tropics

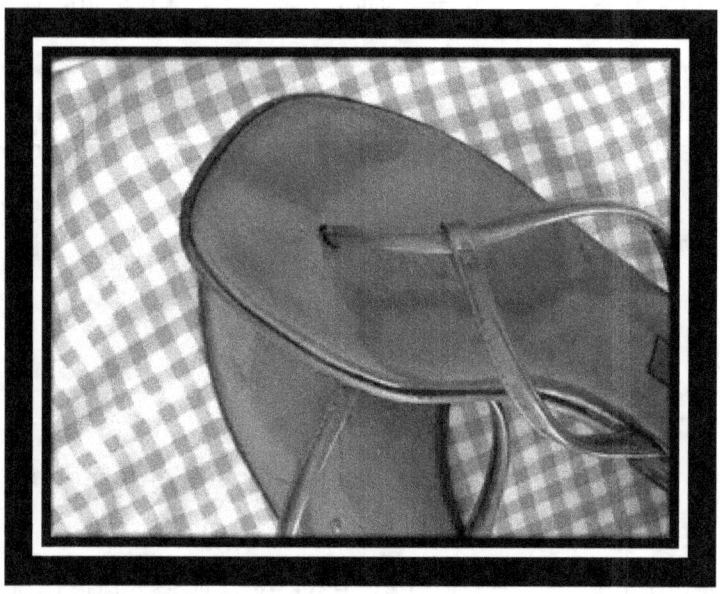

And to think that it is easy and cheap to make sandals. Interestingly, we make good leathers in Nigeria, which is the main raw material. Other materials like sole, buckles are easily available.

You do not need costly machinery to start up. A leather sewing machine, smoothing machines are the major machine needed. Others are knives, tables, and scissors.

An eye for fashion and creativity is the natural endowment needed. If you have not learned the trade, you will need to hire some people to help you out. In any case, if you want to make sandals in large enough quantity to make you rich you will need extra hands.

You do not need an office for a start; you can begin in one-room apartments and supply your customers from there.

To stand out from the average shoemaker in town, your products have to be neat. This way you will also be able to compete with imported ones.

MARKETING: You will need to use distributors to sell your products for you on commission. Use a catchy name as a label for your products.

You have to use a name that is fashionable, short, and easily remembered. Remember names like Gucci, St Michael, Copperfield, etc.

94. Seminars.

You can conduct seminars on topical issues you are proficient in. Seminars to Coop Societies, Local governments, State governments, Schools, Research Institutes, Companies, etc.

This does not involve much cash, as they will mobilize you in most cases.

You may not even be very knowledgeable in the area as long as you have the contact to get the jobs.

You can source resource persons from higher institutions. Jimoh Ibrahim, the head of NICON group, started making his millions from seminars. He made use of his professors to do the talking while he counted the money.

You send your proposal to the organization of interest.

The proposal must contain information about your setup and the promoters, the topic, what the organization will gain by doing the seminar, the resource persons coming, financing, the organization's involvement and your own.

Would it not make sense to have some big men as promoters of the company?

Do not drop names, inform and get the approval of anybody whose name you want to use. You never know the other side may cross-check.

They do not limit seminars to those mentioned above.

You can also hold a seminar for the public.

You must have heard some people holding a seminar on electricity generation.

The person who started that idea is a millionaire as I am writing. You too can research a green area and hold your own seminar.

MARKETING. All the points under management consultancy are relevant.

For a public seminar, your best bet is radio advert. If you can afford TV, it is ok but do your cost and benefit analysis properly.

You can also do free seminars to attract people and sell your written products to them.

CAVEAT: Do not hold a seminar you are not properly prepared for. Get real professionals as resource persons.

As for public seminars, make sure what you teach them works.

95. Stock Broking.

Forget about the present meltdown in the economy that has affected the stock market, the capital market will bounce back.

And in Nigeria, it has not even started with less than 200 quoted companies.

The sweet thing is that you do not even have to be a chartered stockbroker to partake.

There are non-stockbrokers making good money in the capital market.

All you need do is to be affiliated to a firm of brokers and you are in business. I know guys in Ondo, and Ekiti states doing well for themselves using this system.

The capital market is not meant for Lagos people alone. As long as these people have to trade in stocks and there are no brokers, those helping them have to be rewarded, and this is where you come in.

I will advise that young graduates get qualified to enhance your chances. The future for stockbroking as a profession is bright.

At old age, your certificate will work for you.

The brokers get about 1% commission on transactions, which you split as the person who brings the business.

You say what is 1% but 1% 0f 10milion is N100,000 and believe me there are people buying and selling in multiples of that.

The reward does not stop at that.

With the knowledge and fund, you can warehouse stock to sell when the price is high.

That is why you hardly see a poor stockbroker.

Many people died intestate with enormous investments. It is the job of the stockbroker to retrieve the stock, usually on a commission basis, and this could amount too much.

Besides all the aforementioned, you can organize seminars to enlighten people.

And God, millions are ignorant of the operations of the capital market, even among the educated people. Up till today, many still confuse it with insurance.

So what does it take you to start? Be educated and have a befitting office.

People cannot give their money to a fleeting person. You are in the financial sector so you have to be corporate.

Like I said earlier, you need to work through a registered firm of brokers. As a jobber, you cannot trade on the floor of the exchange; only the chartered brokers may do that. (As I am tidying up this book, GTB is already N22.75. The market is alive again)

MARKETING. You need a pleasant office and letters of introduction to high net individuals.

You know them in your territory. Personal contact is inevitable.

You can print flyers and distribute at religious conventions to introduce you outfit. Organizing seminars will also help. Join a social club of high net people.

CAVEAT. Do not swindle your clients. Give honest advice and pay them promptly when they are selling.

96. Stationery.

One business that pays very well which we overlook is the selling of stationery.

For sure, it differs from bookshop running as it takes less money to start. I must add however that some people combine both.

A man dealing in stationery sells things like exercise books, biros, pencils, rulers, writing sheets, gums, staplers, and things like that.

They are everyday used products by everybody, not only students.

The sweetness is that the margins are always large and consumers do not seem to care because the unit price is meagre.

It is not unusual to make more than 100% profit on an item. I tell you an example.

There is a particular fluid pen I had been buying for N250 until one day I decided to hag. I got it for 200 and during the course of researching this book;

I discovered that even at N150, sellers are still making more than 100% profit.

No fuss, the game is value and service because even at N100 I was satisfied.

The secret of this business is to site in a proper place. A well-trafficked place at a corner or on a major road.

To expand your range, you can add cold minerals and water.

You do not need any special training to do this business but research sources of materials.
Like all commerce, buy well to sell well.

MARKETING. Location is important. Print flyers and make attractive sign boards in front of your shop. Arrange your materials neatly and dust-free.

CAVEAT, Study your area. Get good quality materials not envelopes that will not seal.

Provide security.

97. Suya Spot (Barbecue)

During the course of researching this book, some friends and I were somewhere in the Mokola area in Ibadan.

We felt like supporting our drinks with Suya and the lot fell on me to get it from nearby Sabo.

I ordered for N1000 but as this was being wrapped; two guys arrived and ordered for N3000 worth.

Apparently they were sent by their friends as the lot fell on me in my own group. As they were being attended to, other customers arrived.

Within a spell of about twenty minutes, these guys have grossed about N10,000. I said wao, so these uneducated guys are literally printing money here.

Immediately I made up my mind to work further on this.

Some days later, I was at Gas junction on the way to Akobo in the same Ibadan to study the suya man there.

What I saw was a replica of the Sabo experience. Verdict: Suya joint in the right place is a cash cow.

I am aware that a Southerner may not be able to make suya as the northerners but the Ondos have what they call 'asun' which the southerners can learn.

They use female native goats for this and it is very tasty when done properly. As I am writing, I am not aware of a place where this is done in Ibadan and I move around a bit.

Now, if we have a graduate operating suya spot in each state capital, that will be 36 graduates off the road and I am sure they will employ another 36 assistants for a start.

MARKETING. No need for an advert as long as you set shop in a conspicuous place. If your roasted meat is sweet people will beat a path to your place.

The two guys I referred to above came from Oke-Ado, a distance of about 4 kilometers if not more. Learn the trade and get your own special recipe to give you a unique taste and could be the beginning of a takeaway chain that can spread over the globe.

Now add class to make you different and unique.

Let the place be well lit, introduce music, and have some chairs for your customers.

Show off your education to your customers when the opportunity presents itself, they will respect you the more.

CAVEAT, Maintaining a high level of hygiene is necessary. Slaughter healthy animals and do not buy animals the source of which you do not know so as not to buy stolen goats.

98. Website Designing.

With More Nigerians getting into www, the business for web design will expand.

The rate of expansion will be so explosive in the years to come as more people are getting into it and that is why it is being treated separately from other internet businesses.

This is how you will know. Only one or two out of ten people you pick at random can browse.

Two, there are many supposedly enormous concerns you would normally expect to be on the web that is not there.

Some existing sites are nothing to write home about. The other day, I went to one site of a big organization only to meet a black page.

What does this tell us? As more Nigerian get internet literate, many websites will be opened and they will improve many of the existing ones.

Having a site is not the end.

You will need to add or subtract information as things change in your organization and to make it more beautiful.

These are the jobs of a website designer.

To be proficient, learn from excellent ones on the field.

This you will supplement with the software you get on the internet.

Please do not deceive yourself, there is no way you will design a site like that of Intercontinental Bank without learning from the masters.

And you do not go to UBA to say you want to work on their site unless you can convince them you can make a better site than Zenith.

Your customers are everywhere, right from the nearest business to your house.

The problem is that you will need to convince them of the usefulness.

Let them know it is not so expensive and please charge reasonably.

The other day, one came to me talking about hundreds of thousand, I just dismissed him.

MARKETING. On a beautiful letterhead, introduce your outfit in not more than a page, saying who you are, what you are doing, and how it can benefit them.

Do not forget to mention those you have worked for and follow up personally.

Advertise in the papers as you can get a job anywhere in the federation. Another weapon is to show them the ones you have done. Pictures are more powerful than words.

Dress well and be faithful to your promise. After-sales service is important. Check the site yourself and suggest improvements.

99. Writing.

Look, there are tons of money to be made in writing. It had always been like that, and it will continue.

You do not have to be a communication graduate, however, some training in writing will help. Take one online. You can start and learn. In a storm, pray to God but row to shore.

What we are saying is that you do not have to be a Reuben Abatti of the Guardian or an Akinlotan, the Palladium of The Nation, or even Sam Omatseye of the same newspaper.

As long as your readers get the message in correct grammar, you are ok. That is communication, simple. Sunny Ojeagbese has built a communication empire writing simple English.

His story is one that should inspire you. He is the boss of Complete Sports and Success Digest Extra and more.

This is a business he started with just N6,500 twenty-five years ago.

Four thousand of this from the sale of his cameras and N2500 from his mentor.

Today, he sits atop an empire that dashes brand new cars away in prizes.

You can replicate that but if you ask him, he will tell you., you not only have to be committed to your goal, you also have to persevere, be persistent, radiate love among other qualities common with any genuinely successful people.

You ask me what to write on? I will tell you because that is the essence of this book. Let us go.

1. CHILDREN STORIES AND POEMS. Niyi Joseph finished at UI and has never worked for anybody but himself. Today there is hardly any private school in Ibadan where his books are not read.

He may not be an Otedola yet, but he is making a decent living writing storybooks and poems for these schools. All publishers of repute around here respect him.

What stops you from doing the same in your state and even all over the country?

The thing about this is that you do not need big grammar. Simple and correct English telling a story that teaches morals will do.

Please do not tell me there is a lot already on the field because if you think like that you have lost the battle before you start. Remember the world itself is about competition. Write an excellent one and market it well.

2, SPEECH WRITING. Believe me, the speakers do not write some of those speeches you hear on the floors of the assemblies.

Anyway, it has to be like that because many of them are not academically qualified to be there and hear we must hear them.

These people will pay you to write moving speeches for them on topical issues.

Think about a topic that interests Nigerians and consult them.

Look, what do you expect a Modern Three certificate holder to say on the floor at Abuja if he does not have a consultant like you.

I know because I have had an offer like that.

Therefore, if you can write a good speech, in this political era, you can make a kill. It will be easier if you are a member of the party the person belongs to.

Now, do not get me wrong, even the president has speechwriters. That means you can even write for educated politicians if you are so gifted.

3. SCRIPT WRITING. If you have the talent to write plots, you can make a decent living by writing scripts for our fledgling film industry.

You do not have to be as good as Hadley Chase or Professor Akinwunmi Ishola to write a good script.

Those are at the very top and there is enough room in the middle. I must warn that you must be more than average to get good value for your work.

Write a good script, take it to them and you will be handsomely rewarded. Be careful, very careful, people may steal your idea. Dogs eat dogs you know.

4. CONTINUITY PERSON. A continuity man is the secretary of film locations and sets. You take a record of the proceedings to assist the Director.

For this, you need a lot of concentration, as your job will be to provide the missing links from your records. Do it properly and you will be rewarded.

5. NEWSPAPER COLUMNIST. You say not possible and I say it is possible. Introduce a new angle and you are there. I will give you an example.

The students' section in The Nation is a soaring success but tertiary education had been with us since the forties. What are others looking at?

There are three laws in making money. Creativity, creativity, and creativity. During the glorious days of Daily Times, there was this column called Wakaabout in their Lagos Weekend written in adulterated English.

The column had a very wide readership.

I may be wrong but I do not think any newspaper is doing that now. You see, it is not even in Queens English and people loved it.

Give the editor a refreshingly different angle and you have a column.

6,

PAMPHLETS. *Have you ever bought pamphlets like common errors in English or the quotes of great men?*

If you have not, I have and you know, in most cases I bought out of an impulse not necessary out of need.

Most little value purchases like this, the marketers will tell you are made out of impulse.

You can join them and make your own cut. Think about a different angle. Ok, you do not have any, what of writing on the laws of football.

Several times people argue on referee's decision in the premier league out of ignorance. Write out the laws for them and the arguments will abate. I have given you an example think hard you will get more.

7. SPECIAL JOURNAL. Tell me, who is writing on Agaric, and under this, you have a fishery, piggery, poultry, and so on. What of health, if there are, they are not enough. Education is also there and a host of others.

Look, any serious person is looking for knowledge, provide it right and you are there. You could start with free copies as advertisements will defray part of the initial cost.

Ask Obazu Ojeagbese, he will tell you, he went back home with many unsold copies those early days but today his Complete Sports is next to The Punch in circulation.

Commitment and perseverance are words.

8. WRITING OUT POPULAR SONGS. As I am writing this, there is a Bob Marley CD playing on my Laptop. You won't believe it if I tell you the songs are almost all wrongly titled.

Stop the train is titled Love light shining and wait for this, Stir it Up is titled Cheer Up and yet I bought.

Now people will pay you if you correctly write out Maley's songs and even Marvin Gay's in a pamphlet. If nobody else buys, I will.

9. COOKERY. Are you good with food recipes? Even if you are not, you can learn and sell your Knowledge. All you are reading here I researched.

I did not bring them from my mother's womb.

Yorubas want to know about Igbo food and the Hausa lady married to a Yoruba man wants to know about Yoruba food.

Who says continental dishes won't appeal?

10. TEXTBOOKS. You say there are enough textbooks and I say not enough. When A1 English came out, there were more than many English texts on the stands, and the author, Ashade made his money and he is still making it.

The book is still selling today because it is good, damn good. It is selling in as far a place as China.

I, for one, have bought three copies and I am going to buy another one tomorrow for a friend's son I am mentoring. Four copies in one family alone.

Ashade does not hold a doctorate, the secret is that he approached the English Language problem for SSC students from a refreshingly different angle.

I hope the guy writes on English for managers because many managers need such a book. I know, because I have been among managers and I can tell you some are very deficient in the English Language.

We are expecting yours on Chemistry, Biology, Economics, and others. I do not know who Woods is but I know all Accounting students read his books. Give us one evergreen like that and you are made.

11. WRITE FOR AMAZON. Go to Amazon.com and see how people are raking in tons of Money from Writing.I am compiling a book and writing for Amazon.

See one of my books here:
https://www.amazon.com/Amazing-Uses-Baking-Never-Knew-ebook/dp/B089RH3P24

100. Adult Education.

At Gbagi market here in Ibadan, there are hundreds ready to offer a limb to read and write.

There are thousands of them scattered all over the country and they have the money.

This business may not sustain you, but you can add it to remedial school for extra money.

You promote it the way you promote schools by using flyers and posters in an area where you know potential students are.

Some of them may ask you to come to them.

In fact, most of them will say so. There is nothing bad in that, you go to their children and they are ready to pay.

For those who are ready to attend, you set up classes for them, usually in the evenings.

You can use public schools with special arrangements. The bottom line is your fees.
Those teaching matured rich people have to be patient.

Therefore, one has to be mindful of the type of people employed to do the job.

When you are well established they will surprise you, the amount of money it fetches you.

Apart from money, you know people, which is goodwill.

101. Bees Farming.

Bees produce honey. Of all the things created by God, honey arguably has the most medicinal value.

A spoon of original honey every morning will send those little ailments scampering.

The problem is how to get the original honey that is 100% pure. Many of the products you see are adulterated and those do more damage than good.

The market is vast. In fact, if people know that your honey is pure, the distributors will take your entire product.

The present supply cannot meet the demand because few are into it. Honey also sells internationally.

Producing honey needs a lot of commitment and you have to love the job. If your honey is pure, you have a ready market in teaching hospitals and the public because the use is extensive.

Producing honey is a specialty.

You cannot jump into this as you will do in selling beer but the reward is worth it. To do it you have to learn.

Learn not from these N3000 seminars but from a practicing farmer.

It is worth it because as they say, what is worth doing at all is worth doing well. My brother, you do not do bees farming in the city but do it well, the city people will come to the bush to find you.

I know of a retired person in Oke Ogun area of Oyo state making cool cash from this business.

Apart from the land, which you will lease, you need some specially constructed boxes and equally specially made overalls to visit the bees hive.

MARKETING: The business is self-promoted. A distributor with a wide network can take all your honey.

So if you have two or three of them, you are ok. Two or three hospitals can take all.

CAVEAT. Please do not take unnecessary risks, talk to experts. Do not adulterate your product because people will know and it will kill the business.

Please read Honey distribution.

102. Driving School.

Start a driving school. It does not pay much, but then you can use education to make the difference. Take it to them, at home, in the offices. Do not wait for them.

More people are buying cars and many more are desirous of knowing how to drive. In most cases, those buying cars for the first time are green and would have to learn.

Ladies, in particular, will need to learn from outsiders, as the husbands may not be patient enough to teach them. As said, you can pick them up at their places of work and drop them off after training.

Be a patient driver to teach and besides; Be at home with the rules. Your outfit may have to be registered with the government depending on your area.

This business may not make you very rich, but it will fill some financial holes. For a complete lesson, you may charge as much as N20,000 depending on which place you are.

Getting the driving licence for your students is part of your job at a fee. After passing out, follow up on the phone to see how they are progressing, they call this after-sales service and it will surely bring you many referrals.

MARKETING. Brand your vehicle with your driving school name. Also, put a board on top. If you have an office of your own, have a signboard in front.

EXCELLENT DRIVING SCHOOL
(Know How To Drive In 5 Hours)

This is no exaggeration. What it means is the person will drive after 5 lessons of 1 hour each, and many people can easily achieve that feat.

CAVEAT. Do not start a beginner on busy roads.

Do not leave learners on their own, unless you are satisfied with their proficiency.

The tendency is always there for learners to think they know more than they do. It is important to have a brake pedal on your side to stop the car in case of an emergency.

103. Interior Decoration.

Good biz if it inclines you. Cut your own from the rich decorating homes, churches, offices, lying in the dead's state.

Some combine it with cake making. Please see cake making. They are sometimes combined together.

104. Networking /Multi-Level Marketing.

People are making money from networking, also known as multi-level marketing (MLM).

You have heard Tianchi and the rest of them.

The latest in town as I am writing is Quest net.

They deal with exotic jewellery, Technology, and wellness products. Under wellness, you have the bio-disc and pendant.

I must confess I dislike it so much, but then what difference does that make.

I don't have to like it to make it an excellent business. Therefore, if it suits you, go for it.

105. Recharge Cards

If there is no money in this then there is no money in any business. I am not talking about hawking.

Get into the printing and sell to the hawkers.

There are people teaching how to print recharge cards and learn from them.

I can send you the info free if you are interested. (This may soon be out with wider use of internet marketing) Perhaps too late.

106. Trade School.

Apart from aluminium fittings, no other trade is being learned in Ibadan and Lagos and I guess the story is the same all over the country.

Yet in my area about 1-kilometre square, there is no single plumber.

The bricklayers you see are not trained, mostly they are those who went to buy the shovel and gauge, having served as laborers to bricklayers for some time.

The reason people are not learning the trades, I guess, is because there is no class attached to the training. In addition, technical colleges are not enough.

In some places, they are not even available.

People are setting up private polytechnics and Universities but nontechnical school, which will cost less.

You can start by leasing a building running courses like Plumbing. Electrical Engineering, Instrument Engineering, Electronics, Sign Writing and Refrigeration.

 They will be trained for a period of three years before graduation when they will be issued certificates.

Get approval from the government, but you can start running and seek approval later.

If you want to make the kill, train towards the attainment of a certificate recognized by the government. The courses I have mentioned do not need much instrument to teach.

Plumbing, for instance, needs no more than a wrench, dicing machine, some spanners.

The advantage is that, should you win a contract and there is no reason not, your students will be your labour, free of charge.

How much to charge depends on the educational advancement of your area and the economic activities and demand.

Definitely, it will cost more to run a school like that in Lagos than in Kaduna or Umuahia.

Please do not fool yourself that such schools have to be in the city. With a wonderful advertisement, people will come. People send their wards to A-Level School at Offa, Kwara state.

Liaise with trade school teachers for curriculum and resource persons.

MARKETING. You need a good advert on Radio and Paper to let people know there is money in trade learning, more than riding Okada.

They will be self-employed apart from many job opportunities.

You may need to give free seminars on careers in secondary schools to sensitize the young ones that one can do well in life without attending universities.

CAVEAT. Add class. Your own must differ from the backyard workshops.

107. Transportation.

I shudder why educated people do not partake in transportation when it is so clear that the business is lucrative. An educated person will only do it better.

In addition, people should stop turning their noses and stop seeing these jobs as degrading, as master's degree holders will be lucky to get the job of a cab driver in London.

If you doubt me, ask your brother in the UK. If he is sincere, he will confirm my statement.

Transportation business vomits money like a faulty gaming machine and it is on the first day.

If a young graduate gets a N800,000 imported used car today, with careful management, he will pay back within a year.

In Lagos, a sound cab will bring in N5000 a day after expenses. In other cities, it could be less but it is still business. In Ibadan, I am sure a sound cab will bring in N4000 daily after expenses.

The minibuses do not perform less.

Our problem is that we see transportation as the work of touts. Go in there, make your money, and make a difference.

They will respect your education as you will be able to enlighten them on many issues.

I must add that transportation is not restricted to commuting. Goods movement as different from moving people about is part of transportation.

I will explain. A one-ton open truck at Mile 12 market in Lagos or Bodija market in Ibadan Or Central Market in Kaduna will net N4000 naira a day working out at about N120,000 a month. It cannot be less.

How much do they pay at ZENITH that you want to die looking for work you will not get. If you have a truck in a place like a plank market, you can easily kill two birds with a stone.

Learn the plank trade when your vehicle is not on the road. Within two years, you are a plank dealer and a transporter. What is sweeter than that?

Let us face it, apart from the edge which education gives, are we economically better than transporters?

I know one guy here, about 35 years with about 10 vehicles and a four flat building and he is just growing.

People who want to make money have to put away their pride.

I am not advocating that you should be one of them in behaviour or appearance.

God forbid, but you can still be a driver and be corporate.

Take that from me. The man who drives the queen of England is still a driver. Got what I mean?

Getting into this biz has no formality.

Get the driving licence, procure your vehicle, and attach yourself to a park you want to ply and you are off.

The park officials will ask for some money but if you handle them properly, they can defer payment till you have made some money.

You ask where you get the money for the car.

Many parents will be happy to source N800,000 for their unemployed graduate if he chooses to be gainfully employed.

Many have such an amount in their savings and are still doing N50,000 a month job, working 7 to 5.

With good planning and discipline, this business can get to be an octopus in a few years. Short of an accident, you cannot lose.

MARKETING. You do not look for customers, they look for you. Be civil, treat your passengers nice.

CAVEAT. Watch who you carry. Do not be too smart; insure your vehicle comprehensively at least in the first year. Remember, speed kills and destroys transport business.

108. Used Cars.

With the rising costs of cars and a ban on cars older than 5 years getting into the country, the market for used cars will expand.

There is no special education needed for this job except that you have to love cars and know a bit about car repairs.

We are saying this because, one, you must know what you are buying and two, you may need to touch up some cars before you put them on the stand.

If you do not have this skill, you can have a mechanic as a friend or take one as a partner.

To make a good profit, buy well. You must know the cars.

By this, I mean by merely igniting the engine and raving it, you must be able to determine the condition of the engine of certainty.

Bodywork is equally important. Sometimes, the condition of the body will determine how much you pay.

You cannot sell used cars in one corner in your residential area. Locate on a major busy road. There is no alternative to this.

The price depends on what you bought. In this business, be friendly with fellow dealers, as they will bring customers to you when they do not have the cars needed by their customers.

For deals like this, there is usually a commission they collect, which you have to factor into your price.

Sometimes, people will bring cars to you to sell but at other times, search.

I know some people in Ibadan who go to the interiors of Osun and Ekiti states to get used cars and good bargains they get.

You will also be friends with government auctioneers to buy from them when auctioning. Unless you are buying, people giving cars to you to sell will have to wait until after the sale.

MARKETING. Your stand is your best advert. Arrange your cars neatly and wash them up now and then. Be neat yourself and be courteous to callers.

When you make a sale, follow up with a call to ask how the car is performing.

If there is anything you can do, do it cheerfully. Such a customer will recommend you to others. I do not have to tell you it is part of your job to perfect the papers.

If your customer needs accessories such as battery and extra tires, it is your job to get them for him at good prices, which have your own little commission factored in. It is also your responsibility to recommend all other things that will make your customer enjoy his car.

CAVEAT. Do not deal with rickety cars, they fetch little, and besides; they take useful space.

Do not rip those who give you cars to sell. Be satisfied with the agreed commission or agreed price.

109. Used Clothes Selling:

Bend down boutique is a gigantic business, check it out, the lady walking in front of you may put on one.

Add some class into the selling and you make money.

Get a shop in a well-trafficked place. Do not let them bend down let them sit down. Make the shop beautiful with coloured bulbs.

You will need a generator set as our electricity is not reliable.

Racks and hangers must be used to arrange the clothes neatly. Clothes look better under the light.

Most of the used clothes are imported, so, until you have the money to import, you have to go to the importers to buy.

They have locations in all big cities. Most practitioners in Ibadan go to Lagos to buy though. Occasionally traders combine money to send one of theirs to reduce cost.

The business is very lucrative as you can make 200% gains on an item. When you make a purchase, some of the clothes may need dry-cleaning.

Either you do the dry-cleaning yourself or you give the job out. Whichever way, it enhances the value of the cloth.

Torn ones have to be mended you know.

Buying cheap is the secret. You must buy cheap to make a good profit so get to the source.

MARKETING: A neon light signboard in front of your shop is imperative. You may also use local radio and newspaper if available.

Be nice to those who enter your shop.

CAVEAT. Buy well so you can sell well. Your shop must be very secured

110. Vegetable /Okra Gardening:

When I was in a higher institution, I read a book that sounded like making a million on a plot of land doing vegetable gardening throughout the year.

What the writer was saying is that one could be rich in cultivating vegetables throughout the year and he tried to show how to do it.

Because I was spending somebody else's money, I did not bother.

Now that some people are spending my money, I considered the idea, and I researched it.

My findings?

The man was right. It is amazing the amount of money one can make through this medium, but unfortunately, we ignore it. During the dry season, it is a goldmine.

All you need do is to find a site close to the river and a water pump. If you cannot get one, you can use watering cans.

If you have the money, you can do it where there is no river by having a well.

We can do this business in the village provided it is accessible by road.

The sellers in the city will fight one another to buy your products.

Vegetable sellers from Ibadan go as far as Ekiti state to buy vegetables.

I swear, one dry season practice on an acre of land will get you a Tokunbo car.

Some of these vegetables mature in 21 days and as you harvest them you replant.

No serious weeding. You just walk through and handpick. If you live around Festac in Lagos, you must have seen them.

Do not be deceived by their dirty clothes, they are making good money.

No overheads as the sellers come to the farm. Vegetable gardening may not be as profitable in the raining season as the supply is abundant. Some even get vegetables where they did not plant.

Make the little you can make during this period and make the kill during the dry season.

The idea is to farm it throughout the year. If you do not have the knowledge, you can tap from the practising farmers at little or no cost.

Please see the pumpkin for marketing and caveat.

111. Wheat Flour.

Nigerians are on the fast lane.

They want things done for them and want things done quickly.
In those days, mothers used to buy plantain, dry it, and grind it
to flour.

Today people do not have time.

They want it in ready-made flour. You have seen Semovita,
semolina but I want to tell you the mother of them all. It is wheat
flour, very nutritious to both old and young.

The processing is easy. Sort the dirt and small stones out. Grind
and sieve.

Babies can consume it as pap, and adults can convert it to solid
food as you do semovita.

The only thing that may discourage you is the removal of the
small stones. I think there is a way out of this.

Soak to let the small stones settle at the bottom and redry.
Look, this is a big business if you can do it.

The southerners are not used to it yet, but you can introduce it.

Start little in your area and if you are mobile take it to the offices.
Before you know it, everybody will be singing your name.

You can get wheat to buy from big foodstuff markets like Bodija
in Ibadan and Mile 12 in Lagos.

When you are ready to go real commercial, you will need to go to its source, the North. Initially, you do not need to buy the grinding machine, you can contract the grinding out.

MARKETING. Your packaging has to be very attractive with your address and phone number boldly written.

It should be made of strong material so it does not burst with handling. You have fore bearers, copy them.

CAVEAT, please, this is food, do not compromise hygiene. Initially, NAFDAC may not worry you but as you progress, get it approved. Do not get scared off because of them, start first.

112. Men Hairdressers.

I deliberately left out ordinary hairdressing for some reasons. Principal among them is the fact that there are many women in the business.

If a girl drops out of school, she goes to learn either dressmaking, which they call fashion designing or hairdressing. There are so many that you will get one in any five shops.

The result is that they are not making much, which is made worse with erratic electricity supply.

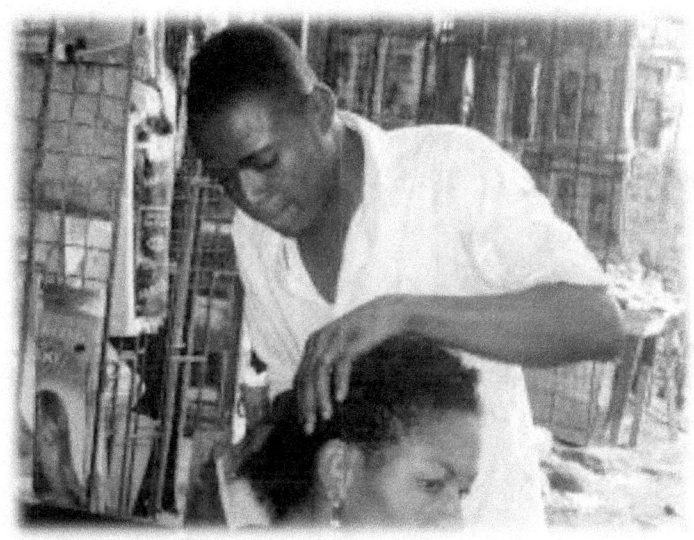

Another one I left out is a patent medicine store. It is lucrative but like all women do it.

I have always believed that a man in a woman's business will probably do better. Curiosity will make the opposite sex want to have a trial and this increases sales if the guy is courteous and proficient.

I have seen very successful men tailors clothing ladies and in this hairdressing business; I have seen saloons, successful salons, with men stylists.

Therefore, when I saw the story below in Success Digest extra, it was a straightforward decision for me to cull it for this book.

You too can make a success of the business as Andrew has done, even if you are a man like Andrew.

Read Andrew story among the inspirational stories.

113. Goat Selling.

Please see cow. See Pit fattening. See Ram fattening.

They are similar.

114. Pig Fattening.

As I am writing this one of my clients is building a 5pen pig fattening pens in Ikire, Oshun state.

He is going to fatten 50 piglets to 100kg per one by December 2023.

None will die, since we are buy winners and we expect a sales revenue of 2.5milliom with about 1.5M profit.

A

kilogram of life pig is now N1000.

This is one business that can never fail unless there is African swine fever epidemic and in that case, it is a disaster.

But it doesn't happen often.

If you do not have money for cement blocks, use bamboo for the wall and palm fond for the roof.

Nothing spoil. However, the floor must be hard.

You must use concrete cement. If the floor is not strong the pigs will injure themselves as their hooves will dig holes on the floor.

Get your seeds from a reputable farm and be sure their father and mother are big breeds.

If you buy the offspring of a rant pig, no matter how well you feed it, it will not grow big.

I have not asked you to do the other type of piggery where you rear sows to produce piglets.

It is lucrative too but it won't bring money on time, besides it is more tedious.

In this one, just feed and feed.

When siting your piggery, water is very important. If you cannot guarantee regular supply of water don't venture into this business.

You either sink a borehole or you site near a river.

If you have a well, ensure it gives enough water and you must get a pump to make the job easy for your farm attendant.

MARKETING. Buyers will beg you to buy. There are boys whose business is to buy and take to other parts of Nigeria. In addition all gala makers use pork.

115: Your Business A Name.

I have attended to this separately because daily; I see people making the mistake of giving their businesses unfitting and unprofessional names.

Most of the time, they arrive at these names out of sentiments.

Agreed your spouse and children are important to you just as I also agree that your religion is important but so also is money. You cannot function well in your mosque without money.

Therefore, I advise you to divest your religion from the naming of your businesses. I am saying this because I have seen Hallelujah primary school; I have seen Rise and shine bread; I have seen Modupe Oluwa food canteen.

They all have their reasons for naming them as such but they are all out of the context of professional business naming. They are just sentimental village people.

If I were deciding on a school to enrol my child, I would prefer a school named Future Leaders or The Achievers to one named Hallelujah even as I shout Hallelujah every day as a Christian.

The last does not sound as if the owners know what they are doing. Similarly, I will prefer my wife does her hair at Exquisite Saloon to Iya Bolu beauty salon.

The woman has named the saloon after her child for sentimental reasons.

The Eleganza group belongs to the Rasaq Okoya lineage.

Were their patriarch to name it after his sons he would have changed the name ten times over.

It just does not gel, it is not business-like.

There are basic things you have to remember when naming a business. Some of them are.

>It must be easy to remember

>It must be short

>It must reflect the business

>It must reflect the value the customer will get

I will analyse two business names to make it clearer.
However, before that, you must understand that naming a business is never by accident even as I agree that the heavenly father may talk to you about it in your dream.

Naming a business is always planned. Some companies contract it out with a large sum of money.

The Yorubas say you act according to your name; this is also true in business.

Now let us analyse the two business names.

ELEGANZA. Without a doubt, this name for the business dynasty of the Okayas meets the four criteria.

It is easy to remember; it is short, just a word, it reflects the business, elegant biros and flasks, and so on.

It is also saying customers will get elegant products and services.

Good corporate name.

TANTALIZER. Another smart one. Short, easy to remember.

You unconsciously have a feeling that it is nourishing because you immediately think of the consumer getting tantalizing meals.

Look around, you will see more examples.

116. How To Choose The Name.

Get 5 well thought out names as I discussed above and let at least 10 people rate them for you on a scale of 1 to 5.

For example, if I like the first name best, I award five marks and one mark to the one I like least. In the end, you add the marks and use the one with the highest mark as your business name.

That is the simplest way to do it.

Do not include your family members in your sample. They will naturally want to lean towards you and that will be biased.

117. How To Write A Business Plan.

Success in business comes as a result of planning. You have to have a detailed, written plan that shows what the ultimate goal is, the reason for the goal, and each milestone that must be passed in order to reach your goal.

A business plan is a written definition of, and operational plan for achieving your goal. You need a complete but success tool in order to define your basic product, income objectives and specific operating procedures.

You have to have a business plan to attract investors, obtain financing and hold onto the confidence of your creditors, particularly in times of cash flow shortages... in this instance, the amount of money you have on hand compared with the expenses that must be met.

Aside from an overall directional policy for the production, sales effort and profit goals of your product--your basic "travel guide" to business success...the most important purpose your business plan will serve will be the basis or foundation of any financial proposals you submit.

Many entrepreneurs are under the mistaken impression that a business plan is the same as a financial proposal, or that a financial proposal constitutes a business plan.

This is just a misunderstanding of the uses of these two separate and different business success aids.

The business plan is a long-range "map" to guide your business to the goal you have set for it.

235

The plan details the what, why, where, how and when, of your business.

Your financial proposal is a request for money based upon your business plan...your business history and objectives.

Understand the differences. They are closely related, but they are not interchangeable.

Writing and putting together a "winning" business plan takes study, research and time, so don't try to do it all in just one or two days.

The easiest way to start is with a loose-leaf notebook and writing materials. Once you get your mind "in gear" and begin thinking about your business plan, "10,000 thoughts and ideas per minute" will begin racing through your mind...

So, it's a good idea when you aren't actually working on your business plan, to carry a pocket notebook and jot down those business ideas as they come to you...ideas for sales promotion, recruiting distributors, and any other thoughts on how to operate and/or build your business.

Later, when you are actually working on your business plan, you can take out this "idea notebook", evaluate your ideas, rework them, refine them, and integrate them into the overall "big picture" of your business plan.

The best business plans for even the smallest businesses run 25 to 30 pages or more, (it could be lesser) so you will need to "title" each page and arrange the different aspects of your business plan into "chapters." The following format should help.

Title Page
Statement of Purpose

Table of Contents
Business Description Market Analysis Competition
Business Location
Management
Current Financial Records
Explanation of Plans for Growth
Projected Profit & Loss/Operating Figures Explanation of
Financing for Growth Documentation
Summary of Business & Outlook for The Future
Listing of Business & personal References

This is a logical organization of the information every business plan should cover. I will explain each of these chapters titles in greater detail, but first, let me elaborate on the reasons for proper organization of your business plan.

Having a set of "questions to answer" about your business forces you to take an objective and critical look at your ideas.

Putting it all down on paper allows you to change, erase and refine everything to function in the manner of a smoothly oiled machine.

You will be able to spot weakness and strengthen them before they develop into major problems.

Overall, you will be developing an operating manual for your business...a valuable tool which will keep your business on track, and guide you in the profitable management of your business.

Because it is your idea, and your business, it is very important that YOU do the planning.

This is YOUR business plan, so YOU develop it, and put it all down on paper just the way YOU want it to read.

Seek out the advice of other people; talk with, listen to, and observe, other people running similar businesses; enlist the advice of your accountant and lawyer...but at the bottom line, do not ever forget it has to be YOUR BUSINESS PLAN!

Remember too, that statistics show the greatest causes of business failure to be poor management and lack of planning...without a plan by which to operate, no one can manage; and without a direction in which to aim its efforts, no business can attain any real success.

On the very first page, which is the title page, put down the name of your business-PETRAGOLD NIGERIA LIMITED--with your business address underneath. Now, skip a couple of lines, and write it all in capital letters: PRINCIPAL OWNER--followed by your name if you are the principal owner.

Examples: PETRAGOLD NIGERIA LIMITED
1,PETRAGOLD STREET, LAGOS ISLAND, LAGOS, NIGERIA.

PRINCIPAL OWNER: Your Name
That is all you will have on this page except the page number - 1- Following your title page is the page for your statement purpose.

This should be a simple statement of your primary business function, such as We are a service business engaged in the business of publishing and selling business success magazines.

The title of the page should be in all capital letters across the top of the page, cantered on your last draft—skip a few lines and write the statement of purpose.

This should be direct, clear, and short—not usually over two or three sentences.

Then you should skip a few lines, and from the left-hand margin of the paper, write out a sub-heading in all capital letters, such as

EXPLANATION OF PURPOSE.

From, and within this subheading you can briefly explain your statement of purpose, such as our surveys have found most entrepreneurs to be "sadly" lacking in basic information that will enable them to achieve success.

We estimate this market at over 20 million persons, with at least half of these people actively "searching" for sources that provide the information they want, and need.

With our business, advertising, and publishing experience, it is our goal to capture at least half of this market of information seekers, with our publication MILLIONAIRE MAGAZINE! Our market research shows we can achieve this goal and realize a profit of #2,000,000 per year within the next 5 years...

The above example is the way you should write your" explanation of purpose," and in subtle definition, why you need an explanation. Point to remember: Keep it short. Very few business purposes, explanations justify more than a half-page long.

Next comes your table of contents page. Do not really worry about this until you have the entire plan completed and ready for final typing. It is a splendid idea though, to list the subject (chapter titles) as I have, and then check off each one as you complete that part of your plan.

By having a list of the points you want to cover, you will also be able to skip around and work on each phase of your business plan as an idea or the interest in organizing that phase, stimulates you.

You will not have to make your thinking or your planning conform to the chronological order of the "chapters" of your business plan—another reason for the loose-leaf notebook.

In describing your business, it is best to begin where your statement purpose leaves off. Describe your product, the production process, who has responsibility for what, and what makes your product or service unique—what gives it an edge in your market. You can briefly summarize your business beginnings, present position and potential for future success.

Next, describe the buyers you are trying to reach. Why they need and want or will buy your product. And the results of any tests or surveys you may have conducted.

 Once you have defined your market; go on to explain how you intend to reach that market, how you will entice these prospects to your product or service and induce them to buy.

You might want to break this chapter down into sections such as, Publicity and promotions, advertising plans, direct sales force, and dealer/distributor programs. Each section would then be an outline of your plans and policies.

Moving into the next chapter on competition, identify who your competitors are their weakness and strong points, explain how you intend to capitalize on those weaknesses and match or better the strong points. Talk to as many of your "indirect" competitors as possible, those operating in different cities and states.

One of the easiest ways of gathering a lot of useful information about your competitors is by developing a series of survey questions and sending these questionnaires out to each of them.

Later on, you might want to compile the answers to these questionnaires into some form of directory or report on this type of business.

It is also advisable to contact the trade associations and publications serving your proposed type of business.

The chapter on management should be an elaboration on the people operating the business. Those people that actually run the business, their job, titles, duties, responsibilities, and background resumes.

It is important that you "paint" a strong picture of your top management people because the people coming to work for you or investing in your business, will be "investing in these people" as much as your product ideas. Individual tenacity, mature judgement under fire, and innovative problem-solving have "won over" more people than all the astronomical sales figures put together.

People becoming involved with any new venture want to know that the person in charge. The guy running the business knows what he's doing, will not lose his cool when problems arise, and has what it takes to make money for all of them.

After showing the "muscle" of this person, go on to outline the other key positions within your business; who the persons are you have selected to handle those jobs and the sources as well as availability of any help you might need.

If you have been in business of any kind, the next chapter is a picture of your financial status, a review of your operating costs and income from the business to date.

Generally, this is a listing of your profit & loss statements for the six months, plus copies of your business income tax records for each of the previous three years the business has been an entity.

The chapter on the explanation of your plans for the future growth of your business is just that: an explanation of how you plan to keep your business growing, a detailed guide of what you're going to do, and how you're going to increase your profits.

These plans should show your goals for the coming year, two years, and three years. By breaking your objectives down into annual plans, your plan will be accepted as more realistic and be more understandable as a part of your ultimate success.

Following this explanation, you will need to itemize the projected cost and income figures of your three-year plan. It will take a lot of research, undoubtedly a good deal of erasing, but it is very important that you list these figures based upon thorough investigation.

You may have to adjust some of your plans downward, but once you've got these two chapters on paper, your whole business plan will fall into line and begin to make sense.

You will have a precise "map" of where you are headed, how much it is going to cost when you can expect to start making money, and how much.

Now that you know where you are going, how much it is going to cost and how long it is going to be before you begin to recoup your investment, you are ready to talk about how and where you are going to get the money to finance your journey.

Unless you are independently wealthy, you will want to use this chapter to list the possibilities and alternatives.

Make a list of friends you can approach, and perhaps induce to put up some money as silent partners.

Make a list of those people you might be able to sell to, as stockholders in your company.

Make a list of relatives and friends that might help you with an outright loan to furnish money for the development of your business.

Then search out and make a list of venture capital organizations, pick up the loan application papers they have.

Read them, study them, and even fill them out on a preliminary basis. And finally, check the costs, determine which business publications would be the best to advertise in, and write an ad you would want to use if you did decide to advertise for monetary help.

With the listing of all the options available to your needs, all that's left is to arrange these options in the order you would want to use them when the time comes to ask for money.

When you are researching these money sources, you will save time by noting the "contact" deal with when you want money, and by developing a working relationship with these people.

In your documentation section, have a credit report on yourself. When you get your credit report, look it over and take whatever steps are necessary to eliminate any negative comments.

Once these have been taken care of, ask for a revised copy of your report and include a copy of that in your business plan.

If you own any patents or copyrights, include copies of these. Any licenses to use someone else's patent or copyright should also be included. If you own the distribution, wholesale, or exclusive sales rights to a product, include copies of this documentation.

You should also include copies of any leases, special agreements or other legal papers that might be pertinent to your business.

In conclusion, write out a brief, overall summary of your business- when the business started, the purpose of the business, what makes your business different, how you will gain a profitable share of the market and your expected success during the coming 5 years.

The last page of your business plan is a "courtesy page" listing the names, addresses and phone numbers of personal and business references, persons who have known you closely for the past five years or longer, and companies or firms you've had business or credit dealings with during the past five years.

And, that is it, your complete business plan. Before you send it out for formal typing; read it over once a day for a week or ten days. Take care of any changes or corrections and then have it reviewed by a Lawyer and then an accountant.

It would also be an outstanding idea to have it reviewed by a business consultant serving the business community to which your business will be related. After these reviews and any last-minute changes you want to make, it will be ready for formal typing.

Congratulations, and my best wishes for the complete fulfilment of all your dreams of success!!!

(Emmanuel K. Olorunfemi wrote this article on Business plan
Esq of MoneyIQ, email— money_iq@yahoo.
We have used this with his permission.

118. Financial Discipline.

The chances are that many of the youths would just be like I was during and after my NYSC. My income was just taking me a week to blow.

There were always excuses to make.

The salary was small; I was used to spending big in England as a government scholar and things like that.

And this was true because as the government was giving me money, my mum was sending money, good money and I was working part-time. So the money was coming, and I was smoking and drinking it away.

Now that is indiscipline in the worst scenario. If I had had a wider view of life, I would have done very much for myself then.

If you cannot manage N5000, you cannot manage 5 Million and that is the truth. A man who cannot save should forget about being rich because even if you put him in the CBN vault and ask him to help himself he will end up a beggar.

If you are starting a business, you cannot afford to spend like a guy who has made it or even a salary earner who has nothing at stake.

Surfing the internet, I stumbled on the write-up below about financial discipline.

I followed it, and it has been better for me. I advise you to do likewise.

Cut down what you are already spending on. You can't start a business being in a financial mess.

Cash Flow is more important than revenue.

And you need to have lots of cash flow coming from your pockets if you will succeed.

Here are some things you can cut down on

• **SMOKING**–if you can't quit, just cut down on a few sticks

• **ALCOHOL**–booze can drain your finances faster than a running tap

• **NIGHT OUTS**–spend some nights at home thinking about making more money

• **GAMBLING**–if you plan to gamble, it is better to gamble in a business

• **VACATION AND COUNTRY CLUBS**–you won't die without a few memberships

• **FOOD**–eat healthily and you can even think clearer

• **LAZINESS**–The biggest thing that will hold you back!

PROCASTINATION. Dangerous disease. Do not allow it.

LIKE THE JONES. Do not compare yourself with anybody, Do not want to be like them. The only time you can copy is a successful business model that will upscale your business.

Most important of all, don't buy anything that constitutes a liability.

A liability is anything that takes money out of your pocket no matter what they are worth.

Think in terms of cash flow. What can I invest in today that will give me funds tomorrow?

119. How To Source Capital.

Let me tell you right away that there is no specific way to source funds because your situation will decide how and what and where.

The banks are not very ready to give loans to their existing customers, let alone a fresh one.

And I say this is wrong. There is no reason a person with a wonderful project should not get help even without collateral, as long as the project can pay back and the borrower has finance discipline.

All hopes are not lost. Things are changing. With the present reforms by the CBN governor, Nigerians may wake up one day and find out they can source funds easily.

So your best bet yet is still yourself or your immediate family.

Many graduates have parents with 3 or 4 cars in their garage. Such people should not find it difficult to raise a couple hundreds of thousands to start off.

I assure you, if you can convince your father about a project and he is sure-footed on your financial discipline, he will fling his only car to kick start the business.

I know because I am a father and I have sold properties to give my children an excellent education. There is no hope to spend rifts who have no respect for money.

A good project can also get sponsors from people you don't even know. Like your parents, he wants to know that you are serious; the project is buoyant, it can repay itself quickly and above all, he can get a good profit.

Like I said somewhere in the book, nobody does business because of God, they do it only for profit.

If Dangote donates 5 Million in a place, it is because he is expecting business to vomit that and more in profit from the place or he is consolidating a hold.

Both will increase his group profit. So package your product and get introduced to high net-individuals who are interested in such a project. If it is profitable enough, he will finance it.

Novel ideas will attract investors more quickly than ideas in an already saturated fields. No investor will rush into soap manufacturing with you and even pure water.

The markets are saturated, except you are attacking it from a refreshingly fresh angle.

The black tablet soap, for example. Go to green areas.

Let me warn you about ambition.

Do not start big, so that if there is a problem, you can cut your loss quickly and stand up again.

Big objects crush under their weights. Even behemoths like Guinness do not hit the entire country at a time with a product.

The smaller it is, the more appealing it is to a financier, and the more serious he thinks you are.

Nothing is bad with starting small, the wise men support it.

They say do not test a river with your two feet. They also say you do not eat an elephant in a piece; you eat it piecemeal.

Learn from them.

Besides, history is on your side.

The big ones, all of them, no exception started small. It is the law of nature.

You can also get support from organizations. For now, you can get in touch with Grofin and livewireNigeria.

Reach them on http//livewire_nigeria.org/about.html . Google for them and more.

You can also get help on the internet. Get into forums. Now, there many collateral-free loan lending companies on the net.

There are many loan apps out there, search for them

There are finance apps now that lend you as much as 500k without collateral.

Try and move with people who are better than you. They will pull you up.

I wish you well.

120. You Will Sacrifice

If anyone tells you the road to the top is easy, do not believe him. It has never been, and it will never be.

Look at all the influential men in history; they sacrificed to get to the top.

Do not get me wrong. You will not be offering goats and rams in one fetish shrine, but you have to make personal sacrifices to be anything worthwhile in life.

Money people can lend you, advice you will get, workers are plenty but one thing nobody can do for you is self-denial.

And this is a vital ingredient to make the success soup.

Those who do nothing become nothing.

If a woman wants to have a baby, she must be prepared to lose blood. You cannot make an omelette without breaking eggs.

There are no two ways about it.

Even in Economics, they say you cannot have everything. You arrange your wants in order of priority or preference; get some at the expense of others.

They call it opportunity cost; I call it a sacrifice. You have to forgo so many things to grow your business.

When starting off, you cannot afford to spend money like an established man.

You cannot attend all parties, and your spouse cannot buy all dresses in fashion.

If, for instance, you are starting a beer joint, you cannot afford to be drinking like a fish; otherwise, you drink yourself out of town.

Thomas Edison is arguably the topmost investor.

He was reported to be working at his lab until very late on a daily basis and did that till 74 years of age.

Nobody says you should not have a rest.

As a matter of fact, if you do not come apart you will fall apart but it is doubtful if Edison would be remembered so much as we do today if he had spent his time in disco halls.

Chie Obafemi Awolowo, first premier of western region and leader of the Yorubas once said that when his peers were busy following women of easy virtue, he was busy working at solving Nigeria's problems.

Is it a wonder then that his name is still the most respected name in the history of the Yorubas?

If he was busy running after wine and women he would not have made such an impact.

You have to give something to get something.

Dr. Sunny Ojeagbese, the boss of complete sports and unarguably the father of Internet marketing here, locked himself up for weeks to decode internet marketing.

During those weeks his wife was the only person to see him and only to bring his meals. That sacrifice has today produced many internet gurus in the country.

I can confess that the little I started with in internet marketing I got through his seminars.

To make good grades in school, you sacrifice your sleep. To be a top athlete, you spend hours in the gym and on the field. For an hour delivery, the motivational speaker must have spent hours collecting his materials and even practising delivery.

For God's sake, you do not become a medic if you have not spent seven years in the university.

If you want to be a chartered accountant you write ICAN examinations and if you want to put on the wig you have to go to law school.

You do not do any of those without self-sacrifice. You must have burnt a lot of candles in the night as they say; you must have shunned many night parties and outings.

Chances are that you will lose friends along the way. These are necessary sacrifices and denials.

People want to ride jeeps without effort. They want to live in mansions without corresponding input.

That is why there are many internet rats spoiling the image of the country. It never happens. Something has to give.

This is the law of nature. You cannot reap where you have not sowed. You must sacrifice.

Go and learn from an average Igbo trader. He sacrifices a lot to grow his business. He sleeps in his shop when he can afford a room. He cuts outings and shuns ostentatious living.

He buys a bike when he can afford a car and when he eventually buys one he buys a beetle when he has a fund for a Benz.

He does all these to grow his business and before you know it the guy has shops all over the place.

Go and do likewise.

121. TWO INSPIRING STORIES THAT WILL CHANGE YOUR BUSINESS MINDSET FOR EVER.

I did not write these true life stories, but stumbled on them and think aspiring businessmen need to read them.

They are old stories but true and very relevant till today.

The first is about a jobless graduate who built his house starting with Okada on instalment.

The second is Andrew man who made his fortune weaving hairs for women.

I gave credit to the writer at the end of each story.

Happy reading.

1.Graduate Okada Man Builds N6m House.

I am a Nigerian from Sapele in Delta State.   I used to be one of the Nigerians that wonder how it would be possible for them to be landlords in Nigeria because of the state of the economy.

Things seemed to go from bad to worse and the hope of ever owning a house of my own could not be imagined at all.

But it got to a time i thought about what to do to help me survive here in Lagos. I realize that making excuses that I graduated from the University and did not get a job after six years will not help me.

At a time I started calling my elder brother in Holland in Europe to get me documents to check out of the country. From the response i was getting from him, I knew to wait for him to come back and help me would remain a pipe dream.

Initially, it was about survival. I needed to get something doing to survive. The guy I was squatting with, though is my cousin, and was tiring of taking care of me. I could feel the pains he was going through to keep things going in the house then.

As fate would have it, one day a tenant in the house I was staying bought a motorcycle, the one they call 'okada'. He is a close friend of my cousin and said he wanted to give it out for commercial, to be working for him.

After we prevailed on him to "wash" the bike for us, that is to buy us drinks in celebration of the purchase of a brand new bike, I also followed him to the licensing office to register the motorcycle.

Thereafter he went to a friend to draft an agreement for him for the bike to be given out to somebody on a higher purchase basis. Here in Lagos they call it "balance and carry".

In the agreement, I discovered that he was requesting for N130,000 (One hundred and thirty thousand naira) from the purchaser for the Bajaj Boxer 5.

Another schedule in the agreement stipulated a payment of N6,000 (six thousand naira) weekly to the owner of the motorcycle. This will continue for six months, after which the said motorcycle would be duly paid for and all documents of the motorcycle handed over to the hire purchaser.

What baffled me in the whole agreement was that everything pertaining to the motorcycle with regards to safety, security, maintenance, renewal of particulars remained the responsibility of the purchaser within this period of six months.

In August 2004, I reviewed the situation of my life and decided to be using the okada since there was no job forthcoming.

Our people say half bread is better than none. My cousin initially objected to the idea of me becoming an okada rider after all these years studying Chemistry in the university.

We knelt down together and prayed to God to protect me on the ever-busy Lagos roads from reckless drivers and I took my destiny in my own hands.

Some people jeered at me that I ended up an okada rider after graduating as a chemistry student from the university. But I was not going to them to beg for anything. At least, I was not stealing. What I was doing is a legitimate business to make ends meet.

My brother, I was committed to my okada vocation. Within five months I paid him all the money and collected the documents of the bike from him.

Having mastered the terrain of okada business, I put in more effort to make something out of it.   Within six months, again I bought another brand new BAJAJ Boxer 5 and also gave it out on balance and carry basis.
.

I give God the glory as we speak I have 23 Okadas here in Lagos which people use to work for me. What I did was to look for space and put a caravan on it as my office where they come and balance money to me.

From the proceeds from my okada ventures, I bought land in Mowe in the Lagos, Ogun state axis after asking so many questions and carrying out investigations on the real owner of the land. I did not want to lose my hard-earned money to land speculators.

The whole negotiations kicked off at the Baale's compound and the land touts in that district of Mowe are controlled by the Baale. I paid N320,000 for the land because it is not too far from the expressway. But now no land is less than N800,000 in that area.

I must confess to you it is not an easy thing at all to build a house, but with God all things are possible. The Architect I went to do the design and charged me so much money. I had to go to my uncle in FESTAC Town, Lagos to collect his Architectural design to build my house.

On-site I had a foreman who knows how to build a house. We call him an engineer. But I am sure he trained somewhere. I am always on-site with my okada to check what they were doing there.

The road leading to the house was very bad. So many at times the vehicle bringing building materials to my site would break down.

The land touts issue in Mowe is not bad as people tend to paint it. It is just a matter of understanding and cooperation. They will tell you what you have to give to them at every stage of the construction.

It is only when you refuse to pay and start to quote the law that you will have problems with them. They can even enter your site in the night and bring your building down. Yes, they could be that ruthless.

In my case, I made sure I settled them through the Baale so that they do not bring their trouble to my site. So far, I have funded the house through my okada business.

At the end of every month, I put a percentage of the proceeds into the building project. It is a house of two flats of 3 bedrooms each. I have completed the building and moved in. I can say I am truly fulfilled.

It is like a joke to me that I am now a landlord. It is amazing. My cousin who was living in a self-contained apartment was still paying rent doing a white-collar job.

But here I am a landlord.To reciprocate his kind gesture of keeping me in his apartment in Ojodu Berger area of Lagos, I gave out the second flat to him to be living in.

So that he can also plan from my house to build his own house. I did not have savings in the bank before embarking on the building. That is where most people miss it.

Arrange your finances properly and with what you have. It is a gradual process, I have spent over N6 million on the building. What is left now is the painting of the outside of the building.

The inside is already painted. I used quality materials all through the building. The next thing would be to perfect all the papers, this I have already started with the Ogun State Government.

CREDIT. (This article was written by Debo Adejana(www.deboadejana.com was culled from success Digest Extra)

Now go and do likewise.

2. Andrew Became A Landlord, Weaving Women's Hair.

It all started as a joke when I was honest with me, to face the reality of life. Before I was braiding women's hair, life had thrown me some unexpected setbacks, having searched for a job in Lagos for seven years with my B.Sc. degree in Sociology.

At a time, I became a member of the free readers association, always going to Ogba Bus Stop to flip through the newspaper every morning instead of buying as others do. All I needed to do was just to pay N20 to flip through the papers.

But at one time, I discovered that this habit was gradually turning me to a public commentator to know if there was vacancy anywhere.

Commentator and analyst of national issues. Whoever wanted to know recent events in the country would come to me where I used to sit at the balcony of the house where I lived with my cousin. Poverty can cause a lot of things.

Imagine somebody just paying N20 and he has access to all the national newspapers in the vendor's stand. The vendors also like the idea because they make a lot of profit from the patronage of free readers.

 So many people liked the idea because they make a lot of profit from the patronage of free readers. So many people like me did not have N100 as we sold newspapers a few years back.

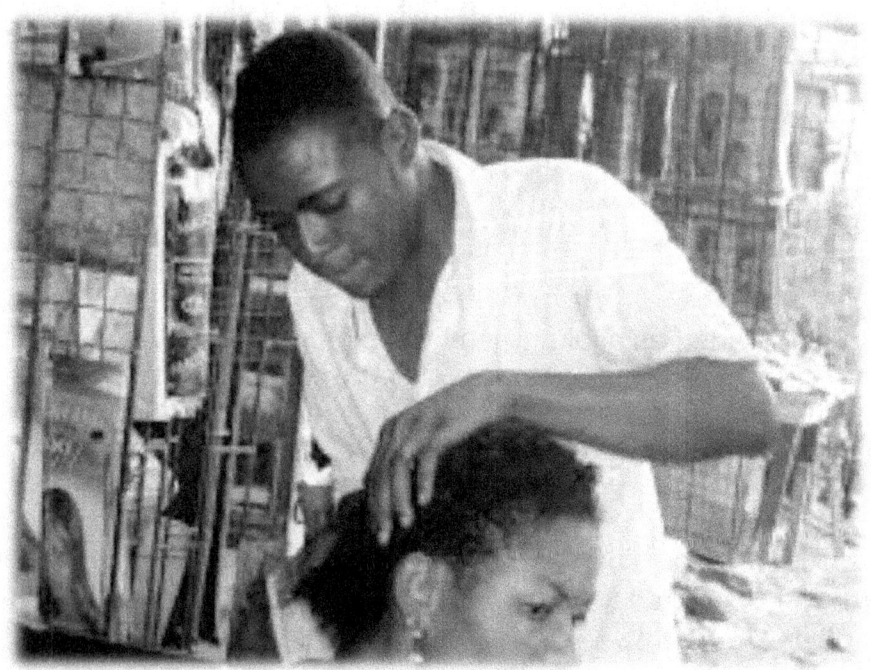

Sometimes, the job opportunities and vacancies published in these newspapers do not lead anyone to gainful employment. When you get there, the number of people will embarrass you.

They will tell you they only need five people out of the thousands of graduates that applied for the job.

It was at this point I allowed my brain to function to help me out. The only alternative I had was to take my destiny in my own hands and move forward from where I was as an applicant in search of a white-collar job.

After this long search for a job to no avail, I thought of starting my own business that I could build into something substantial, I got started by establishing a barber's shop on College Road, Ogba, area of Lagos.

 The next step I took was to seek help from people who could facilitate my business. But the help was not forthcoming; I had to concentrate on the haircutting business to survive. I started with just two clippers.

Fortunately, I had a customer Mr. Ben that was always coming to cut his hair in my salon. We call him Ben O. One day, he came and was in haste and wanted urgent service but there was no clipper to barb him.

He asked me why I could not buy more clippers to take care of the teeming customers now trooping to my salon. I explained my condition to him. He promised to lend me some money to rent a better and larger shop.

I thought he was joking, two months later, he loaned me N150,000 to rent a shop and equip it. It was like manna from heaven. That was how I started Diamond Salon, big boys and girls started coming into cut their hair. I got three more guys to work for me in the salon.

The real business started when Lady Celia, who normally comes to the salon told me I could do more things in the salon- like weaving women's hair, perming, and retouching their hair to make more money.

 She directed me to a place at Surulere where I could go and learn more about the business, types of hairs, styles, and right shampoos for different types of hair.

For instance, if you have oily hair and want to use a conditioner, we help you to choose one that is made for oily hair.

This issue of hair type, style, colour, perms, relaxers, treatment took me a whole year. But the real challenge was my ability to weave hair myself. I had to learn it because I realized it was a money-spinning venture.

After I was through with the training I made my salon very attractive and had air-conditioners and flat-screen television installed.

Believe me; Nigerian women spend money on their hair. We charge N1,500 to weave or braid hair, N700 to fix weave-on; if it is just setting and retouching it is N400.

When I look at what comes to me some days of the week, especially weekends from the salon, I thank God that I took the bold step to go into the business.

My father used to tell me there is no royal road to success. Some of my colleagues who jeered at me when I started the weaving business tagged me "woman wrapper", they would say the "guy don kolo", and poverty has finished him. But today I have many things to show for it.

One day, one of my customers told me she had two plots of land at Odoguyan in Ikorudu, Lagos that she wanted to sell for N400,000 (four hundred thousand naira) I told her I was interested. I inform my aunt who is a lawyer to help me to prepare the necessary documents to purchase the land. That was how I bought the land.

Sometime in June 2007, a Pentecostal Church here at Ikeja had a program. They wanted to come out with a unique, uniform hairstyle.

The favor of God came upon me and I was contacted to bring my men to fix their weave-on. We charged N700 each and the women were more than 2000. We finished the job in 3 days.

I paid the guys I had trained and went to start my building. I ordered building materials like hollowed blocks, trips of sharp sand, granite, and laterite to do the filling of DPC and the building of the house. That was how the process of building two units of flats of three bedrooms each began.

Before I knew it, the Lagos State government official of the Ministry of Physical Planning in the local government came to mark the building, claiming that the building had no approval. I did not know what they meant by approval.

I was livid with anger when they told me what was involved to get approval for the building. How can the government collect such money from me, a young man struggling to build a place to hide his head?

There was nothing I could do. After "God. it is "government". They can come and demolish the building. I had to comply with dropping money on every table at Alausa to move my file from one office to the other. The approval came out after eight months.

Ikorodu land touts too are something else. The government should do something about them. They dealt with me before I complied to pay them N25,000 for foundation when I wanted to roof the house they came to collect N30,000 from me.

Imagine that they said they bought the electric poles and I paid another N10,000 for that. I did not make plans for these expenses.

Building experiences is something a man should have. It does not go the way you think. At a time a lady customer loaned me N180,000 to pay the workers that came to do the decking for me. I intend building on top since I had the approval of a story building.

Right now I am living on the down floor, everything concerning the fitting and finishing is ready on the down floor. I will be giving out the second flat to a tenant very soon. By the time the price of cement comes down, I will start the building of the story building.

As I share the joy of becoming a landlord in Lagos with you, I am still owing the Architect and Mr. Kunle, the engineer that did the structural design for me to get approval for some money.

The thing is that those that built the house did not look at the structural design one day. But those in government insisted I must do it.

When I moved into the house, these aluminum-sliding windows were not fixed. But I did not want to continue to live as a tenant and be paying rent. But everything is ready on the ground floor. I used quality materials and I am happy to be living in my own compound."

Did I hear you say what exactly are you waiting for?
I really think you should hit the ground running. You can call in for help. To your success!

CREDIT. (This article, culled from Success Digest Extra was written by Debo
Adejana an Estate Consultant(Debo
Adejana(www.deboadejana.com

MY SPECIAL 3

It is not possible for me to have done all the businesses in this book even as I have had first-hand knowledge about them as a management consultant.

But there are three that I have done that have made me money.

I am sure if you struggle to establish any of these here you will never lack money.

I have put them here separately so that you can pay special attention to them and take them seriously.

Happily enough, they don't take much to start, buy if you are well heeled you can start on a big scale, it will only shorten your journey to the big league,

Here we go

1: Piggery.

The only risk in this business is a disease called African swine fever.

A very deadly disease but it comes ones in many, many years. Besides that, unlike poultry, you do not have anything to fear.

As I am writing, a kilogram of live pig is N500, so if you have a 100kg pig, you cash in N50,000 and you can get to 100kg in 6 months.

If you do not have much, you can make the pen with bamboo but make sure, the floor is well cemented so as not to break their legs.

There must be abundant supply of water. A well is not enough unless you do not have many, so you may go and site near a river or brook.

This is the simple mathematics.

If you buy a piglet for say 8k, feed it for 6 months with about 15k, you can sell for 50k.

Do the maths to get the percentage profit. If you do it in the village, the cost of feeding will reduce as you will get roughages from the farms.

Things like pawpaw, vegetables, cassava peels etc.

And you are lucky, pigs eat anything.

2: School.

School is big business. The sweetest thing is that you do not need any raw materials and electricity is not an issue for you. Go and start small and grow.

I own a school and use it to give my children sound education.

Two chartered accountants, a nurse and two bankers. I am not rich but I am comfortable.

This secret I am telling you will never be exposed to you by any uncle or aunt. They will always tell you they are struggling.

3: Drop Shipping.

If you are the city guy and don't want a dirty job like farming then go do Drop shipping.

Simply put, it is importing high-luxury items and sell.

See the car mouse below and the wrist watch.

That mouse came under 1.5k and the wristwatch came under 3k. If you are a good salesman, you can sell that watch for 20k. That is a steal.

If you do not want to do the leg work, open a shop on Konga and Jumia and use face book to send traffic there and make cool money. No man will resist that watch if he has money.

I have shown you the way. If you are not rich, it is all your fault.

INTOUCH WITH THE AUTHOR

You may need to get in touch with the author for assistance. In fact it is your right to do so as a buyer of this book. It is the promise of the author to mentor you to wealth. Therefore feel free to contact him

OFFICE ADDRESS. Future Leaders Building, Omolayo Bus Stop, Akobo, Ibadan.
E-MAIL jidolconsul005@yahoo.com
PHONE 08034241050 09029529555

The author is also a Motivational speaker and Internet professional. He runs an internet school in Ibadan the advert of which you will see elsewhere in this book.

For his services please get across. You will gain tremendously by sending your e mail to us for up-dates.

You will get to the top

Otunba Jide Omiyale

BACK COVER

This book is borne out of three deep convictions. One, that our youths should be encouraged to focus on what they can do for themselves in the form of self-employment.

Two, a conviction that the future of Nigeria and indeed of any country depends on the small and medium size companies and thirdly, properly managed small companies will eventually become big.

Razaq Okoya, the patriarch of the Eleganza dynasty started by selling wrist watches.

Alabukun powder used in all nooks and crannies of this country was started very small. Michelin, the tyre octopus was started by a father and son on a bike.

Inside the book are more than a hundred business ideas which are practicable and profitable, some of which you can even start with Zero capital.

Some may sound weird to you but they have all been tested positive.

Of course, though targeted at unemployed graduates, the book is also invaluable to retirees and salaried people who want to have a business of their own.

Written in such a way as to educate and entertain, it is an attempt to assist in industrialising Nigeria and keeping our youths from the street

ABOUT THE AUTHOUR

Jide Omiyale attended St. Pauls Anglican School, Effon Alaye, Doherty Memorial Grammar School, Ijero Ekiti and Muslim College, Ijebu Ode before proceeding to Nene College, England as a Federal Government Scholar to read applied chemistry.

At Nene College, he won prizes from where he proceeded to read Marketing and later Business Administration.

Having lectured at the School of Chemical technology, Zaria, he moved to join the Michelin group where he was a manager for years. Currently, he is the Managing consultant of Jidol Consul, a management and Internet consulting outfit in Ibadan.

A holder of MBA, a fellow of Chartered Institute of Marketing, Nigerian, Jide Omiyale also belongs to the Chartered Institute of Marketing, England.

He is also the author of Easy Road to Solid Wealth and DO-IT-YOURSELF, a book detailing recipes for more than 20 products you can manufacture at home.

www.ingramcontent.com/pod-product-compliance
Lightning Source LLC
Chambersburg PA
CBHW071031290526
45795CB00004B/1178